Tools for Transformation

Tools for
Transformation

Dr Carol Head

© 2020 Dr Carol Head

All rights reserved. Without limiting the rights under copyright reserved above, no part of this publication may be reproduced, stored in or introduced into a retrieval system, or transmitted, in any form or by any means (electronic, mechanical, photocopying, recording or otherwise), without the prior written permission of the copyright owner.

Disclaimer: The author does not provide medical advice or prescribe the use of any technique as a form of treatment for physical, emotional or medical problems without the advice of a physician, either directly or indirectly. The intent of the author is only to offer information to help you in your quest for spiritual and emotional wellbeing. In the event you use any of the information in this book for yourself, the author and the publisher assume no responsibility.

Publishing Details:

A catalogue record for this book is available from the National Library of Australia

ISBN: 978-0-9942335-2-3 (Paperback)
ISBN: 978-0-9942335-3-0 (Ebook)

Front cover illustration: Emma Gazzard
Cover layout: Pickawoowoo Publishing Group
Interior design: Pickawoowoo Publishing Group
Printing and channel distribution: Lightning Source / Ingram

Author contact:
Website: drcarolhead.com.au
Email: drcarolhead@gmail.com

Contents

Introduction · vii

Part One **Paying Attention** · 1
Chapter 1 Paying Attention to Our Emotions · · · · · · · · · · · · · · 3
Chapter 2 Paying Attention to Our Thinking · · · · · · · · · · · · · · 10
Chapter 3 Paying Attention to Our Physical Symptoms · · · · · · · · 20
Chapter 4 Paying Attention to Our Intuition · · · · · · · · · · · · · · 28
Chapter 5 Paying Attention to the Universe · · · · · · · · · · · · · · 37
Chapter 6 Looking After Our Physical Body · · · · · · · · · · · · · · 43
Chapter 7 Relationships and Connections · · · · · · · · · · · · · · · 48
Chapter 8 Finding Joy and Passion · · · · · · · · · · · · · · · · · · · 60
Chapter 9 Connecting With the Earth · · · · · · · · · · · · · · · · · · 66

Part Two **Transformative Practices** · · · · · · · · · · · · · · · · · 75
Chapter 10 Minimalism/Letting Go · · · · · · · · · · · · · · · · · · · 79
Chapter 11 Reflection, Contemplation and Meditation · · · · · · · · 87
Chapter 12 Opening the Heart · 94
Chapter 13 Living in the Present · 103
Chapter 14 Healing · 110
Chapter 15 Tapping into Source Energy · · · · · · · · · · · · · · · · 115

Conclusion – Life is the Spiritual Practice · · · · · · · · 121

Introduction

THIS BOOK CONTINUES ON FROM my first book, *Holistic Medicine: Beyond the Physical*. It outlines ways we might live a more holistic life and transform ourselves into who we are meant to be. Much of this book is about paying better attention to ourselves – to our emotions, thoughts, intuition, passions and to signs and synchronicities. It is also about paying better attention to the process of our lives, both the joyous times and the hard times, and to reflect upon what is happening in our lives as a means to better understand ourselves.

For readers of *Holistic Medicine*, some of this book will revise the concepts explored in that book, but I look deeper into how we can transform ourselves into the person we are meant to be.

Life is about transforming into our authentic selves, allowing our soul to shine through our body and mind (our physical self) by channelling spirit. In this way, we become whole. These things are not easy to do all the time; we catch glimpses of them when we get in flow. When we are in flow, we are creative and joyful. Everything comes easily to us and it is as if we are living the life we are meant to live. Of course, this is how it should be. We live the life we are meant to live when we operate from a place of soul, open our hearts and allow spirit to move through us.

I find it hard to live from the space of soul a lot of the time although when I write, I usually drop into it quite easily. When I do things that light me up or bring me joy, I can access this space. But I spend much of the time in my head, thinking too much and paying attention to what other people think or say. I operate from my ego and my left brain. So I constantly have to remind myself how to be more soulful.

Holistic medicine and transformation are really just about living from our soul, being authentic to who we really are. When we get into this soulful space, we can heal what needs to be healed. It is a deep healing.

The soul is that part of us that exists outside time and space. Our soul is the ancient part of us that is wise and connected to the rest of the universe and to source energy. It carries memories from other lives, and these soul memories can influence how we behave in this life.

Spirit is a part of soul, but it connects all souls to the greater source energy. When we live from soul, we live in spirit, filled with light and inspired to be the whole person we came here to be.

This small book goes through some ways we can be more aware of when we are not living from soul and how we might access the energy of spirit better. I hope it will help you transform into the whole person you are meant to be.

Part One

Paying Attention

Part One looks at the various ways we can pay better attention to what our soul is trying to tell us. When we are living from our soul, our heart is open, we are in line with source energy and we know what our soul is telling us. But when we get out of alignment and live from ego, we don't always listen to our soul. It is always calling, it is always trying to get our attention, but if we are not open to hearing then sometimes its voice is a mere whisper.

To hear the soul whispers we have to pay attention to our emotions, physical body, thoughts, intuition; to signs and synchronicities; and to finding our joy. All of these things can pave the way to uncovering our soul and its calling.

CHAPTER 1

Paying Attention to Our Emotions

I WROTE IN *HOLISTIC MEDICINE* that we avoid, deny and suppress our emotions and feelings. We have learnt to avoid feeling certain emotions, as society teaches us that logic and rational thought should control our lives. Yet our emotions are one way of our inner self letting us know what is really going on. Rather than ignoring our feelings, it is much better to always pay attention to them.

To do this we must pay attention to when they begin to emerge. When we start to feel some emotion, instead of ignoring it or pushing it away, we let ourselves feel it. We go with the feeling and let it have its way with us. We don't have to act it out in any way or think about it; we just let ourselves feel it in our body and energy field.

When we pay attention to feelings and emotions in this way, they always eventually dissipate. Emotions, whether positive or not so positive, are always transitory if we let ourselves feel them fully. Often, as we feel them, we gain insight into what the feeling is trying to tell us. This is not a logical way of thinking but an intuitive insight into why we are angry or sad or happy. Sometimes, the feeling just comes and goes without us having to understand anything at all.

HOLDING ONTO FEELINGS

I was undertaking clinical supervision recently and it had been a hard week. I had seen too many patients experiencing sadness and grief, and one of my friend's sons had died. All of it weighed heavily upon me and I wasn't aware that I was holding onto the feelings so tightly.

My supervisor advised me to feel it in my body; where was it, what was it like? Initially, it was a heaviness in my heart area, an ache for all the grief that had built up in my life recently. It felt heavy and dark. I let myself feel it for a while and tears spilt down my cheeks. The pain in my heart eased after a while and I felt my heart opening. At the same time, I felt a weight upon my shoulders dragging me down. I also felt heaviness, despair and helplessness, and I tried not to resist feeling them.

I described what I was feeling to my supervisor and she encouraged me to let the feelings move and allow the weight to lift. But my body seemed to have other ideas. I could feel energy flowing down my arms and out through my fingers, so I let it flow. The weight and heaviness transformed into energy, flowing away from my shoulders, along my arms and out through my hands. I could feel it leaving my fingers like electricity. Gradually, it eased up in my right hand but continued to flow through my left arm until eventually, it dissipated. My shoulders were lighter and I felt freer. I hadn't even realised I was holding onto so much emotional stuff. Some of it was mine but I had taken on some of my patients' grief as well.

It is easiest to feel our emotions with the body, for this is where they originate and where they can get blocked. As we feel the sensation within our body, we can become familiar with the feeling and let it have its way. We may cry or laugh or shake. We may find it useful to talk about what we are experiencing in a descriptive way rather than an analysing way. Our bodies may lead us to process the feelings in a variety of ways: letting energy flow from our hands or head or feet, feeling our muscles relax as we let the feeling go, standing up and shaking our arms and legs, feeling our feet grounded to the earth. There are many ways to process the feelings that come to us. Often, we innately know what is the best way for us if we just sit with the feeling and allow our body to tell us what we need.

If we have held onto feelings and emotions for a long time, we may need professional help to process them and a safe space in which to do so. We don't need to remember what caused the feelings to arise. All we need to do is connect to the feeling state and feel where we are holding it in our body. Once we can feel it in our body, we can let the body process it naturally. We don't have to know what it is about or rationalise why we have it or how we should let it go. This is a feeling process, not a thinking process, and we need to try to stay out of our brains as much as possible. We need to stop trying to analyse it all and just let ourselves feel.

After I had let the energy pour out of my hands, I realised that I often took on the burdens of patients without thinking about it, and carried some of their stuff on my shoulders. I didn't have to think about it to let it go. I just needed to allow my body to process it and let it go in the best way it knew. I can now use this technique after I've seen patients whose burdens I try to take on. I just sit quietly after they've gone and feel the negative energy leaving my arms and shoulders.

ANGER

Another feeling I have trouble experiencing and processing is anger. Like most women in our society, I was taught not to be angry, not to feel anger. Men and boys are taught that anger is okay but that sadness and fear are not. Anger is a very necessary feeling. It tells us when there is a threat, when we are being put upon, when we are in danger of losing our dignity or when we are in harm's way.

In one relationship, I was with a partner who was having trouble committing. It was as though he wasn't sure he wanted to be in the relationship, so half the time he was loving and involved and the other half distant and removed. I felt strange stirrings of anger towards him and I couldn't understand why. I would feel it rise in me at certain times and I'd try to push it away. Because I had been taught that anger is wrong for women to express, I didn't want to be angry at him. We should be caring and understanding. I struggled with feeling angry and with loving this man at the same time. Then one day we were on holiday together and he asked me to leave because he was struggling with some issues. As I drove home, I struggled with sadness and anger all mixed in together. By the time I got home, I was accessing the anger and I was mad. I didn't like the feeling but gradually as I allowed myself to feel it, I realised that I didn't like the way he was treating me. This realisation enabled me to change my approach and talk with him about his behaviour. This was a huge step for me and it helped me understand the processing of my feelings much better.

I wish I could have accessed my anger when I was younger. Women are treated poorly in our society and they are angry about it. We have to use our anger to demand change on a personal level and a societal level. We have to get used to accessing and feeling our emotions and paying attention to their messages. Then we have to act upon the messages.

A lot of men have been taught not to feel or express sadness or fear. Yet both these feelings are essential to survival and wellbeing.

When we are sad and we allow ourselves to feel and express this, the tears that we produce contain endorphins that help us feel better. When we allow ourselves to feel fear, we are able to work towards being safe rather than putting ourselves in danger.

Most of us need to do some work around feeling. Most of us have forgotten that feelings are useful signals to what is going on in our lives and that when we feel them and process their messages, they don't build up inside us. When we don't process our feelings, they inevitably affect how we live and may affect our physical body.

TOOLS
BOOKS
The following books are useful when dealing with blocked emotions.

The Molecules of Emotion – Candace Pert. Simon and Schuster, 2012. Looks at the science behind our emotions and investigates why we feel the way we feel.

The Emotion Code: How to Release Your Trapped Emotions for Abundant Health, Love and Happiness – Bradley Nelson. Vermilion, 2019. Provides practical advice and strategies on how to let go of emotional wounds and blockages. We can use these techniques to let go of old emotions, or find an emotion code therapist.

THERAPY
The types of therapy that help with releasing feelings are usually not based on talking therapy. Talking therapy such as cognitive behaviour therapy (CBT) can help with changing thought patterns and behaviours, which can in turn help us feel more, but the therapies

that really get into the deeper feelings are those that deal with feelings and the physical body more specifically. They help us process emotional stuff and release it from our body. This is what we want to do with feelings – feel them, release them and let them go. Many of us hold feelings in parts of our body and this can bring about illness. As we release the feelings, we begin to heal.

Look for a somatic psychotherapist, hypnotherapist or a counsellor who deals with bodywork and processing feelings specifically. Kinesiologists and reiki practitioners can also work with releasing feelings. Any form of physical therapy such as acupuncture, massage, Bowen therapy or reflexology can access emotional stuff and help release it in a safe environment.

SITTING WITH THE FEELING

I encourage you to spend time feeling. Where are you holding tension in your body? Where do you feel pain or heaviness or constriction? Pay attention to the area and feel. Does it bring a picture to your mind? Is there a colour to it? Investigate the feeling with your senses as you really begin to feel it. Then allow yourself to process it in whatever way your body suggests.

Do this as much as you need and pay attention to what else it brings up for you. The feelings may bring up thoughts, intuitive ideas, more feelings or images and sounds.

I believe that when we feel uncomfortable about an issue or person or situation, this is our soul whispering to us about change. Our discomfort signals that something is not right for us. By accessing this discomfort and feeling it, we can usually find a way to change something about ourselves or about the situation.

TRY THIS

Meditations that deal with feelings can be very helpful.

First, get comfortable, preferably sitting on a supportive chair. Make sure you have privacy in a quiet, safe space. You may want to have a crystal in front of you. I find amethyst is good for releasing emotions, as is lighting a candle. Close your eyes and take three deep breaths.

Let yourself relax into the chair. Sit quietly for a few moments and feel your breath rising and falling.

Now bring your attention to your body and feel any areas of tension or unease. Focus on one area for a moment and feel the tension or pain. Does this feeling have a name? Can you identify an emotion connected with the area? Is there an image that comes to mind? Is this feeling associated with an argument or event in your life?

While staying relaxed, explore the feeling in your body. Give it a name and identify where it has come from.

As you feel the emotion and discomfort in your body, bring your hands to the area and let the feeling begin to release. You may want to say something like, 'I release this feeling', or breathe into the area and with each outgoing breath release the feeling and pain. Some people might feel the energy of the emotion travelling out of their hands or feet. Let your body dictate how to release the feeling. Allow yourself some time to do this.

Once the discomfort or pain diminishes, keep your hands there and visualise bright white light or energy filling the area.

Slowly bring your awareness back to your breath, take three deep breaths and bring yourself back to the space. Feel yourself grounded back to the earth. Open your eyes and move a little.

You may want to write down what you have experienced and learnt from the exercise. Give yourself some credit for allowing the process to happen.

CHAPTER 2

Paying Attention to Our Thinking

I WROTE ABOUT THE DIFFERENCES in left and right brain thinking in *Holistic Medicine*.

To simplify this, we can see the left brain as the logical rational side. It uses linear thinking and is the voice in our head. It looks at the parts of a problem and analyses them. It can't see the big picture so well.

The right brain thinks in pictures and images and is nonlinear in nature. It sees the whole picture but can't see the parts, and it thinks intuitively rather than logically.

DOES MEDITATION HELP?

I thought that my left brain was too dominant so I decided that in order to transform my mind, I needed to learn to meditate. I thought if only I could meditate, I could quieten the left side of the brain and access the right better. So for many months I meditated. And I thought it was a good thing towards being a more spiritual being. But eventually I realised I didn't need to do it. I wasn't finding joy in it. It wasn't helping me get closer to the divine. It wasn't making me happier. Or more peaceful. It wasn't doing anything for me except making me restless when I tried to sit and meditate. My inner self was letting me know that I didn't need to do it just because someone else had found it useful.

For a while, I believed that a spiritual person should formally meditate. Now I no longer believe that. I believe that many people find it useful and for them it is a way to get in touch with their right brain, their inner selves and spirit. For various reasons, formal sitting meditation doesn't suit me at the moment. Sitting tends to make my mind more active. For me, walking or swimming or cross-country skiing are all forms of meditation where I focus on movement and align it with breath. It works to calm my mind and I often have flashes of inspiration when I do these activities.

Any technique that helps us let go of unproductive left-brain thinking is useful. Some of our left-brain thinking is used to problem-solve; this is productive. It is the spiral of negative and unproductive thought that we need to identify and step back from.

This thinking usually happens when we are worried or stressed about something. It is the time to let go of thinking and ego and get in touch with our other parts. These spiralling and endless loops of thoughts are just mental clutter, which we ultimately need to clean up.

How do we clean up our mental clutter?

Meditation helps some people but for many, the thoughts come back (if they ever left). To clean up our mind clutter, we may need to look at it more logically. We may need to address what the thoughts are about and why they are there. Are they someone else's thoughts that we have inadvertently adopted? Are they from our beliefs; beliefs that may not necessarily be true?

Wherever they come from it sometimes helps to find their origins. Is it one of your father's favourite sayings? A teacher's offhand remark? Your best friend's comment on your wedding day? Many of our recurrent thoughts come from someone else or from society. These thoughts are part of our culture but we can always question them and decide that we don't need to believe them anymore.

Other mental clutter can be because we have failed to make a decision or a choice about some aspect of our life and we think we are stuck in a situation without choice, when we always have a choice. We can always choose to make a new decision about the direction our life is heading. Once we've made the decision, we need to take some action to reinforce the decision.

Most of us have some negative thoughts circling around in our brain and sometimes, we believe these thoughts are true. But thoughts are just thoughts, not truth or fact. In order to challenge these negative thoughts, we may need to sit down and write them out and look at why we believe them and then why we might not need to believe them anymore.

For some people with persistent negative thoughts ruling their life that they find difficult to challenge, it may be useful to see a therapist. CBT looks at the link between thoughts, feelings and behaviours and can help challenge negative thoughts that often lead to negative feelings and behaviours.

Each of us can investigate our thinking patterns to see if what we are thinking is in fact truth or just a thought. We can change the way we think and feel by challenging and changing our thoughts and beliefs. The simplest way to change our thinking is to reframe what is happening. Instead of looking at our mental clutter as a problem, we can look at it as an opportunity to learn more about ourselves. Mental clutter usually signifies that we are stuck in some way. We are going in circles and are unable to solve the problem.

Paying Better Attention

Recently in my clinical practice, I had reason to look more closely at my finances. I don't know why I hadn't been closely following them before this but as the universe tends to do, it prompted me to take a close look. I had just started a new practice some eight months before and thought things were slowly building, but when I looked more closely it was evident that the figures were pretty stable but not increasing. I wasn't earning enough long term for the practice to be viable.

This put me into a spin and my mental activity increased. I tried to think my way out of the problem using my left brain. I talked to friends and wrote about the issue but remained stuck in my left brain trying to find a solution. My thoughts were going in circles and my head started to hurt. I knew I was stuck in the spirals of thought but for a while I couldn't get out of my own head.

Eventually, I listened to my own advice and took a step back to observe my thoughts. I decided that the lack of income wasn't a problem but an opportunity. It was an opportunity to let go of the thinking and just go with the process. This is a lesson I am still learning. I am learning to trust that my inner self and spirit knows what is going on, and to let go of the need to control the outcome and go with the flow. To use my feelings, intuition and signs from the universe to navigate my way through.

This stepping back from the mind and its clutter is important but it can be difficult, as we tend to get carried away in our own heads. This is where meditation helps many people.

Meditation for me is usually walking, so to help quieten my mind, I went for a long walk. While it often helps, I also have to take a step back and observe my thinking as something separate from my soul. My thinking is not the real me, so I separate it out for a while and look at the clutter and decide to let it go. Of course, at times the thinking creeps back in and I need to reaffirm each time that the thoughts are just thoughts.

The logical brain is very useful for all sorts of problem-solving but when it goes in circles and can't find a solution, it is time to give it a rest and use other methods. The other methods are intuitive and right brained. The solution will come from dreams or signs or synchronicities or inner guidance – gut feelings or sudden hits of inspiration. So I let go of the mental clutter and wait for life to unfold.

As is usual for me, I can't wait for life to unfold so I have a tarot reading. It tells me that the energy around me is stuck and that I can't make a decision at that moment. I have to be patient and let the process unfold. Most of us find this extremely difficult to do because we like to be in control and to plan out our life. But when we are stuck in circles in our head, it is a sure sign that the left brain can't solve this particular problem and we need to just let our right brain, intuition and spirit, lead us to an answer. Sometimes this takes time, sometimes it happens quickly.

Personally, I have more to learn about patience and trust. I try as hard as I can to let go of the outcome and the planning and just see what happens.

The next week at work was quiet and there were not enough patients to make much money. But I was still unclear, so I asked for a sign from the universe about what direction I should take.

I had a meeting with my supervisor who always helps me get more clarity. Speaking with another person who is a trained counsellor about our issues can be very helpful. She helped me see what was happening with much more clarity. I began to see that I had been focusing on GP work as a way to find more meaning in my life and it always came up short. I knew I loved writing but I didn't ever see it as work. Now I could see that the only reason I was working in medicine was to fund my writing. So I could ask the simple question, 'What's the best way to make money so I can write?'

For decades, I had been struggling with work, finding it at times soul-destroying and at other times satisfactory. But it was never something I was passionate about, or that brought me much joy. I had been looking in the wrong place. Writing was what I needed to do to pursue meaning and develop my passion. So how could I best make money to pursue my writing dreams? To a degree, I felt that it didn't matter what work I did. There was no struggle about the type of work, but rather a new realisation that I was just doing it to make a living. I had some resistance to this idea as it seemed that I should be passionate about it, but I realised I could still be good at my work without being passionate about it. It was just the way I made my living.

This shift in my thinking was dramatic but I don't think I would have got there so quickly if I hadn't sat down with a professional and talked it out. My supervisor's skills were a bit like magic drawing the answers out of me. They were in me all along but my left brain was too busy and I couldn't hear them.

I was still waiting for some sort of sign as to which direction would be best for me, but there was no longer the urgency there had been to reach an outcome. I was more able to relax into the process and be patient and wait for further direction.

As I let go of the need to control the outcome and reach a decision, my stress levels went down and my left brain stopped going in circles. I began to access my intuition and realised that I needed to change my work again. Initially, I felt some resistance to doing this as I knew some of my patients would be disappointed if I left practice again. Then an opportunity came up to do a locum in Aboriginal Health and it seemed like the perfect answer. I had to let go of my worries about how my patients would take the news and go with what felt right. So I decided to close my little practice and take the locum work. It would give me more money and mean I could work less and write more. It seemed like the perfect solution and one that I hadn't seen when my brain was going a hundred miles an hour trying to reach a solution.

While logical thinking is great for some things, it isn't always great at change. It can always think of reasons not to change and to stay where things are comfortable. When I start thinking too much, I find that I need to step back and realise that change is upon me whether I like it or not. Then I wait to see what my soul is seeking, and the answer usually comes to me through my intuition or through signs and synchronicities from the universe.

The funny thing was that while I was worried about what my colleagues and patients would think about closing my practice, they were all positive about the changes and the new opportunities that I was embracing. It seems that when we make a soul-led change, everything just falls into place and the mental clutter ceases.

Tools
Therapy
Talking with a trained professional about the swirl of thoughts in your head can often help. They may help you challenge some of your thoughts and beliefs and see that they are just thoughts. They

might help you reframe the negative thinking into an opportunity to change something. They might use CBT to help you change the way your thinking is linked to your feelings and behaviours.

The difficult thing is usually choosing a therapist, and this may be where you need to go with your intuition. Talk with the therapist on the phone and get a sense of whether you connect with them, or book a session and see what they're like. Go with your gut and if you feel they aren't the right person for you, don't be afraid to look for someone else.

Disengaging Your Left Brain

Until you learn how to rest the left brain, you might need to learn how to disengage it from ruminating on the problem. You do this by making it engage on something else, thereby distracting it. Methods of distraction are many and varied but they usually work best if the left brain is given a job to do. Engage it in a serious linear problem and it will generally relax. The left brain does not like trying to sort out nonlinear problems because it can't solve them; it goes in circles and drives itself crazy. Give it a linear problem to solve.

Here are some ways to do that.

Writing all your thoughts down is sometimes a useful way of disengaging your thinking – not trying to solve problems, just recording the thoughts. This is why keeping a journal is so helpful. You can get your thoughts and feelings down on paper without having to judge them.

Alternatively, you can try observing your thoughts. Let them swirl around the left side of your brain without attaching yourself to them. Pretend your inner self is just observing the thoughts as they swirl around. You don't have to stop your left brain from thinking.

Rather, you learn how not to attach yourself to the thoughts. The thoughts are not the real us, they are just our left brain trying to process information.

While meditation is a good way of disengaging the left brain, often when we are in the throes of thinking too much, meditation is too hard. Engaging the left brain in something it likes doing, like word and number puzzles or games, is ideal. The left brain has trouble doing more than one thing at a time, so this activity usually decreases the vortex of useless thinking that we get trapped in.

USING YOUR LEFT BRAIN

While it may seem I am being negative about the left brain, I believe it is a wonderful tool for solving some problems. When it tries to solve a nonlinear problem though it just goes around in circles. Give it a linear problem or get it to work on parts of the problem, and it comes into its own. The left brain is logical and can pull apart a problem, whereas it has trouble looking at the problem as a whole.

Write down the problem, the main issue, and then try to pull it apart by writing down the parts of the problem. This may include feelings and patterns of behaviour. Then take each bit and see if there is something you can do to affect that part or if you just need to have patience and let the process of life occur.

I once saw a patient whose wife had left him. He was caught in a spiral of thinking that was driving him crazy. When he was able to pull the problem apart, he could see that he had a number of issues. He wanted to get his wife to love him again. He wanted to maintain contact with his children. He wanted life to go back to the way it was. He felt angry and betrayed. He was concerned about his finances.

We talked about these issues and what he could do to address any of them. Some of them he had no control over so he decided to focus on the ones he could control. He decided he needed to see a lawyer for advice and a therapist to help with processing his feelings. He had some logical structure to approach the issues and this helped his left brain stop ruminating so much.

CHAPTER 3

Paying Attention to Our Physical Symptoms

OUR PHYSICAL SYMPTOMS ARE GOOD indicators that something is wrong somewhere. Many of us assume that physical symptoms are merely telling us that there is something wrong with our physical body. While this may be correct, it is not the whole story. Our physical symptoms also tell us what is going awry with our energy, with our emotional, mental and spiritual selves. Such symptoms are messages if we can hear them and pay attention.

KNEE PAIN

Recently, I arrived home from dinner and my left knee started to hurt. Within an hour, it was quite a severe pain, which led me to taking some Panadol and going to bed. The pain persisted throughout the night, waking me each time I moved my knee. The next morning, the pain was still there. It was like a burning ache in the medial side of my knee over the end of the femur. It was quite tender in one particular spot and a bit sore and stiff generally. The right knee also seemed to be mildly affected in the morning.

My first thought was that I had hurt it when gardening the day before, but there was no definite injury or sprain. My second thought was that it was something more serious like infection or bone cancer. Of course, we always imagine the worst-case scenario in the middle of the night. When the pain had settled a little later that morning, I decided to take my own advice and pay attention to the messages that my body was sending me.

What did it mean?

The leg signifies something about direction and the left side relates to the spiritual, so maybe there was something about my spiritual direction that I needed to pay attention to? I looked up all my books on the meaning of physical symptoms and drew a blank; nothing seemed to resonate or make sense to me. Then I came across another book I had recently bought. This one refers to the left knee as relating to yang or paternalistic symbolism, and pain in the knee to an emotion, deep feeling or a memory that we are having trouble accepting and integrating into our life and our conscious awareness. While not being specific about the exact cause, this resonated with me.

I had been in the process of trying to bring up and let go of old emotions and feelings related to relationships. I had spent some time working on a particularly painful relationship break-up and felt that I had let some of the stuff go relating to this issue. But maybe I had lots more to let go of?

Surprisingly, once I paid attention to the knee pain on a conscious level and investigated what the meaning was, the knee pain settled.

When an illness comes on suddenly without warning symptoms, it can give us a message to help us change our life before the illness becomes serious, such as a heart attack, a cancer diagnosis, diabetes or autoimmune diseases.

However, all disease and illness has a message if we are prepared to listen to our bodies. A patient I saw many years ago had a heart attack in his forties. It changed his life. He stopped smoking and drinking. He started eating better and exercising. He left his high-powered job and started spending more time with his family and friends. He started to take care of himself and nurture both himself and his connections with other people. He paid attention to the message and the meaning and changed his life for the better. He moved towards wholeness and began paying attention to the callings of his soul. He began to heal himself.

There are many ways to decipher the messages behind symptoms or illnesses. I use various books that look into the meaning behind symptoms, but we can also use our intuition to decipher the meaning. We can look at the function of the part of the body that is affected and draw intuitive conclusions from that. For example, if a hand is giving pain, the hand is used for doing things so maybe something we are doing or not doing is not right for us. This is at a very basic level of understanding but such interpretations can be helpful. We may need more details about the issue, in which case it is useful to look up more information or even see an energy healer or kinesiologist for help.

TEETH PROBLEMS

Recently, I had problems with my teeth on the left side. I thought about what this might mean but I couldn't get to the bottom of it. So I went to the dentist who couldn't figure out why I was having trouble, except that maybe my teeth were cracking. So he fixed a crown onto one of them. A lot of pain and money later, my teeth were still giving me problems, pain and sensitivity. The dentist had no answer. So I decided it must be a message I was not understanding or acting upon.

Tools for Transformation

I looked up teeth problems in my books. Annette Noontil says that the overall concept of the upper teeth is what the plan will be like when finished, seeing the big picture of the plan. The individual teeth are about planning for involvement and discernment of the plan. Because they are on the left, it's about the spiritual aspect. Sounds a bit like a cryptic crossword. The lower teeth are about planning for new experiences, and the affected molar is about being careful to analyse.

In her book, Evette Rose talks about teeth grinding as the unconscious trying to process and resolve deep emotions. While I'm not great with emotional resolution at times, I didn't consciously feel I had emotions to resolve at that moment.

I couldn't work out what was going on. I didn't understand what my teeth were trying to tell me so I let it rest for a while and stopped thinking about it.

Then one day, the teeth really started to hurt and I decided there must be a message for me. The pain made me pay attention. I did the medical things by seeing the dentist and taking antibiotics and the pain gradually settled, but the thought was still nagging at me that there was some message I was just not getting. The dentist thought the teeth were fine so I felt that all I needed to do was understand the message and they would settle completely. It was around that time that I was closing my GP clinic. Once it was all settled, the teeth seemed much better but there was still something not quite right.

Then one of my back molars cracked in half. It wasn't as sore, but the dentist told me I'd need to have it taken out and replaced with an implant. Why were my teeth cracking in half? What was my soul trying to tell me? Was it just a physical cause? Maybe it was due to too much clenching of teeth or chewing too hard?

With all physical symptoms, I believe there is a spiritual cause as well. There is always a message for us in there somewhere. Sometimes it's very hard to work out the message so I have to just sit with it and see what happens. I try to remain open to the possibilities and ask spirit for some guidance.

I had the tooth removed. I became more aware that I was clenching my teeth at night and began to worry that all my teeth would crack. I tried a mouth guard to stop the impact of grinding, but I have a very active gag reflex and couldn't stand to wear one. Except to crown the teeth that had small cracks, the dentist had no answers either. Somehow, I needed to stop grinding and clenching my jaw at night.

I went back to the books and decided to do some work on releasing blocked emotions. I was listening to *The Emotion Code* on audiobook, which gave me the opportunity to begin to process my blocked emotions. I booked a session with an emotion code therapist. As I released blocked emotions, I began to feel more peaceful and started to feel that I was clenching less at night.

The problem with my teeth is ongoing but if I pay attention to the symptoms and follow where the process leads, I begin to take a path that I might not have otherwise taken. The linking of my teeth symptoms with my blocked emotions was a gradual process. If we follow these processes we can use them to transform our lives for the better.

TOOLS
BOOKS
All the following books have useful information about the meaning behind physical symptoms and illnesses.

The Body is the Barometer of the Soul – Annette Noontil. McPherson's Printing Group, 1996.

Heal Your Body – Louise Hay. Hay House, 1984.

Your Body's Telling You: Love Yourself – Lise Bourbeau. Lotus Press, 2004.

Metaphysical Anatomy: Your Body is Talking, are You Listening? – Evette Rose. CreateSpace, 2013.

What Your Aches and Pains are Telling You: Cries of the Body, Messages from the Soul – Michel Odoul. Healing Arts, 2018.

The Secret Language of Your Body – Inna Segal. Blue Angel Gallery, 2007.

HELPING PROFESSIONALS

The best person to see to help you identify what your symptom or disease is trying to tell you is a medical intuitive. These people intuit what is medically wrong with you and the meaning behind the problem. They are hard to find but practitioners who use energy healing such as reiki or kinesiology often have this skill. Use your intuition to search on the internet for medical intuitives local to your area and try them out. Word-of-mouth recommendations are also a great way to find someone who can help.

USING YOUR INTUITION

I will talk more about using your intuition in the next chapter. Many people have great intuition but they don't trust it when it comes to themselves. If you have a specific area of the body that is causing you trouble, you might try talking to it to get some ideas about what is behind the issue. Have a conversation with your uterus or heart, or use the next tool to connect with your body. You can also use writing or another creative process to help you understand things intuitively.

Check out the next chapter for how to pay attention to and trust your intuition.

Connecting With the Body
This exercise helps you connect with your body.

Get comfortable and quiet. Take three deep breaths and centre yourself. Feel the energy of the earth under your feet or body, and the energy of the heavens surrounding you with white light.

Take your attention to your body and tune in to where you might have a problem. Take your focus to this part of the body and pay attention to how it feels or appears. What colour is it? Is it painful, or hot, or cold, or burning, or sharp, or dull, or heavy? Focus on the area. Is there a feeling that comes up when you focus on this place? Is there an image or sound or word related to the area? Let your intuition guide you.

Explore the area fully and follow what comes up for you. If you need to process a feeling, let it out. If you need to visualise, allow yourself to follow this.

As you pay close attention to the area, notice what else comes up. Are there other areas that need attention that are connected in some way?

Once you have explored the area, come back to centre and feel or imagine the energy or light filling your heart, flowing up from the earth and down from the heavens – white light, healing energy or however you like to imagine it. Allow it to fill your heart, then flow to the area of concern so that it becomes full of energy and light. Place your hands on the area and allow the energy and light to flow through your hands into the space. Pay attention to anything this brings up in you.

Once you have bathed the area in light and energy, bring yourself back to centre. Feel the light and energy contract around you and feel yourself deeply grounded to the earth. Take three deep breaths and slowly bring your attention back to the present and to where you are. If you feel dizzy or spacey, take some more deep breaths and feel yourself really grounded to the earth.

CHAPTER 4

Paying Attention to Our Intuition

OUR INTUITION IS OUR SOUL and spirit speaking to us and through us. It is difficult to categorise and capture but it is located throughout the body. It exists in our right brain, in our gut, in our body, in our heart. It is not one thing and there is not just one way of intuiting.

There are four main types of intuition. We all access our intuition in different ways:

- Clairvoyance: clear seeing
- Clairaudience: clear hearing
- Claircognisance: clear knowing
- Clairsentience: clear feeling.

With each, we receive messages through our senses. Most of us use one of these ways as our primary intuitive sense, with sometimes a secondary way. We can also access our intuition through dreams, daydreams and intuitive tools such as tarot and runes.

My primary intuitive sense is clear knowing (claircognisance), which in some ways is the hardest intuitive sense to trust. How do

I know that what I know is my intuition and not my mind? If you're clairvoyant and you see a vision of something, or you hear intuitive whispers (clairaudient), it is often clear that it's your intuition. But people who are claircognisant or clairsentient can have more trouble trusting their intuition. With all of the intuitive senses, it sometimes takes training to trust yourself and the messages you receive.

The Intuitive Senses

How do you know which intuitive sense is your primary sense? For some people it is easy but it can take some investigating for others, especially if you have never trusted your intuition.

Clairvoyance: clear seeing or clear vision. These people will see visions, images and symbols in their mind's eye. Occasionally there will be actual visions but usually clairvoyance is from within the mind's eye or third eye. Sometimes the visions will appear in dreams that foretell the future or reveal something important to the dreamer. People who are clairvoyant usually have a talent for visualising; they can easily imagine in their mind's eye a particular scene or activity. At times it can be difficult to tell the difference between daydreaming and clairvoyant visions. Clairvoyants usually learn best through visual means and enjoy movies and other visual media.

Clairaudience: clear hearing. These people will hear whispers or voices within their mind's ear or they might hear a voice that seems to arise from outside of them. Sometimes this can be confusing and people worry that they are hearing voices that might indicate mental illness. But in clairaudience, the voices are usually clear, comforting, to the point and not rambling. They never tell someone to harm themselves or others. Clairaudient people are often quite sensitive to external noises. They often talk to themselves in their head, having a conversation about how to tackle a problem. Clairaudients usually learn best through hearing and may prefer audio books to the written word. They also usually like to listen to music.

Claircognisance: clear knowing. These people are often logical thinkers who have sudden bright ideas or just know the answer to a problem or question. Usually, the intuition is like a light bulb moment and they suddenly know an answer to a problem, or have a creative insight. Occasionally, the insight comes over time but it nags at them until they pay attention to it. Most claircognisants have a busy mind and they think about things a lot. Often, the answers come out of the blue once they stop logically trying to figure out a problem. A claircognisant person probably likes writing and prefers learning through written sources and books. They like to gather information.

Clairsentience: clear feeling. These people can feel other people's moods and feelings. They are usually very empathic and can feel drained after they've been with a large group of people. They usually have a good handle on what people are like and can detect when someone is lying or being dishonest. They also pick up on both positive and negative feelings in other people. For this reason clairsentient people have a hard time watching distressing news stories or dealing with other people's tragedies; they pick up on the difficult emotions and absorb some of this energy. If you've been told you're too sensitive, you're probably clairsentient. On the positive side, you get strong gut feelings that are usually spot-on. You can read the energy in a room and avoid negative energies. You can tell when people are upset even if they're putting on a brave face and you can be good at caring for other people.

Using and Trusting Our Intuition

With intuition, we need to:

- Use and trust it
- Listen to the messages we receive and act on them
- Begin to develop our inner guidance, which is where we use our intuition, our feelings and our soul's messages to direct our life along the path of soul.

My intuition is sometimes clear so that I just know what to do in a tricky situation but often, my logical thinking brain overshadows my intuition. When I was faced with not knowing what to do about my GP practice, I tried so hard to think my way out of the problem. Deep within, I knew that I needed to make a change but I ignored this inner knowing for a while. I tried to be logical about the situation, weigh up the pros and cons and seek a rational answer. Answers, however, are very rarely simply logical and rational. Answers usually come with flashes of intuition, after which the left brain catches up and can sort out the logical steps towards making a change.

When I finally listened to my intuition that was telling me to close my practice and take a different direction, I was relieved. I thought, 'Ah yes, that is the right decision,' knowing within that it was the correct direction. Then I put my left brain to work to sort out how to make the change. I mapped out the steps to take while at the same time trying to stay in tune with my inner knowing. When something seemed too hard, I would take a step back and tap into my intuition.

Accessing Your Intuition

Tapping into their intuition is easy for some people. Sometimes it just happens spontaneously; you see an image or hear an answer or feel a deep knowing. Sometimes, you need to get out of your left-brain thinking to hear or see or feel the answer. Some people meditate to access it, or pray, or seek an answer from the tarot or the runes or other intuitive tools. There are many ways to tap into your intuition and the more you practise, the better you get at it.

The first step for many people is to identify which intuitive processes suit them naturally and then play with them. Use your intuition to help with small problems at first and as you get better you can use it for bigger problems. Which café will I go to today? What clothes should I wear? Where will I find a car park? Who is that ringing me? Where are my car keys?

If you have trouble identifying which process is your most natural, then you may be someone who uses a variety of intuitive processes. Take your time and explore them. If you're good at visualising, then practise visualising. If you get strong gut feelings, pay attention to them. If you feel nervous around a certain person, take note of that. If you hear a repetitive thought or voice, pay attention to what it is saying.

It's also useful to use intuitive tools. I prefer the tarot, but runes and oracle cards are also fun and helpful. Get familiar with one tool. Use it when you need advice and when you're not getting enough information from your senses.

You can also use your intuition when you're feeling stressed and your left brain is going around in circles. Take a step back from your logical thinking, quieten your left brain and make your mind and body receptive to your intuition. Use your preferred intuitive sense and wait patiently for it to let you know what you should do. Usually, to stop the left brain from thinking so much and distract yourself from the problem, it's good to stop concentrating on the problem and give yourself time and space to let your right brain processes work. The answers may come out of the blue, or gradually creep into your awareness. You may have a pivotal dream or come across a sign from the universe that enables you to understand your intuition.

TRUSTING YOUR INTUITION

Tapping into your intuition may not be as hard as paying attention to and trusting your intuition. Sometimes, it is asking you to do something you don't understand or that your logical brain is telling you is risky. Your intuition is a message from your inner self but sometimes, you don't like what you are seeing or hearing or feeling. Sometimes, these messages from soul demand more than you think you can give.

Yet when you follow your intuition, your life starts to go somewhere special. Following the whispers of the soul brings joy and a peacefulness that you don't get when you follow the loud voice of ego and left brain. These usually tell you what you should be doing. It is often the voice of society and culture that you have been listening to over many years. 'I should be doing this job because I am good at it and I make a good living.' 'I should stay in this relationship for the children's sake.' 'I should go to church because my parents expect it of me.'

There are many 'shoulds' in our lives but when we begin to listen to our intuition, we are often presented with options that we hadn't previously thought about.

Many of us don't trust the answers our intuition gives us. We are so ruled by our logical minds that we simply don't trust something that isn't logical. Learning to trust our intuition is a process in itself.

First, we practise listening to our intuition. Then we start to trust it. We follow it. We take the answers it gives us and act on them.

If you're having trouble with this, you're not alone. Begin slowly. Take small steps. First, pay attention to your intuition on a specific issue. Once you have intuited an answer or solution, check out whether there will be any major disadvantages in trusting and following the intuition. If there won't be, then follow the intuition and see what happens.

Try it for minor things first and see how it works for you. For example, try to intuit who is ringing you. If you have a gut feeling to contact someone, do so and see what transpires. If you sense someone isn't doing so well despite their smile, dig a little deeper and see what they say. If you can't find an item, use your intuition to find it. There are many small ways to begin trusting your intuition so that when you have bigger problems, you can use it with confidence.

When I'm not feeling so confident about my intuition, I use the tarot to check it out further. I pick a few cards that help me sort out what my intuition is telling me. This is often an easy way to help me make a decision. One weekend, I was trying to decide whether to stay home or go to Melbourne and visit friends. I picked the Hermit card from the tarot, which signified to me that I should withdraw and spend the time at home.

When I was thinking about doing locums instead of continuing to run my own practice, I had a knowing that locums was the direction I needed to go in but I didn't trust myself completely. So I drew some cards for each option. The cards for the locum showed me that I would have more time for writing and that I would be happier in the long term. The cards I drew for staying showed change on the horizon anyway, after a period of hard work. I knew more clearly that locum work was the right option.

To trust your intuition may be hard at first but if you take it slowly and cross-check your hunches with the tarot or runes or any type of oracle cards, you will gradually build your confidence. As you practise paying attention and trusting your intuition, you will get better at using it as one of your senses.

It is important when using your intuition to remember that you have a logical left brain as well. While intuitive hunches, visions, voices or knowledge are not arrived at in a logical way, it is good to check out their messages with your logical brain. What will the results of acting in a certain way and following your intuition be? What are the steps to take to make it happen? How will following your intuition affect the rest of your life? What are the pros and cons of different options?

Tools
Helping Professionals
Any person who helps you access your intuition, or who uses their intuition to access a higher wisdom, is a worthwhile investment in time and money. I see a tarot reader when I feel really stuck and need some direction based on intuition rather than logic. Word-of-mouth is the best way to find a good tarot reader or intuitive reader.

Intuitive Tools
I use tarot cards mostly but there are a variety of intuitive tools and it's good to use what most appeals to you. Runes, angel cards, oracle cards and many other intuitive tools are useful ways to tap into your intuition. Sometimes, messages come clearly but if you're stuck, then using an intuitive tool is a great way to let go of the left brain and

access the right side. You just need to trust that the messages you receive are accurate.

TRUSTING INTUITION – KEEPING A DIARY
If you're a bit of a sceptic about intuition, then keeping track of your intuitive hunches is a great way to begin to trust yourself. Record a hunch you have, or do a card reading and then write down how it works out and what the outcomes are.

CHAPTER 5

Paying Attention to the Universe

WE RECEIVE MESSAGES THROUGH OUR intuition and from soul but we may also get messages from spirit and the universe. These messages seem to be external but they are attempts by soul and spirit to help us on our path.

SIGNS AND SYNCHRONICITIES

These spirit-inspired signs and synchronicities are a little bit like magic. They light our path and help us remember that the world is a wonderful interconnected whole.

Sometimes, a series of events will occur that just seem to put us on a certain path. Last year I began work in a new practice and advertised in a local magazine. The director of an aged care facility saw the ad and rang to ask if I would do some work for them. This was fortuitous, as I needed some money so I agreed to work there one morning a week. When I arrived to work there, the clinical nurse manager took me on the round of patients and we hit it off. I have been working once a week since then and earning some much needed extra money.

My friendship with the nurse manager has blossomed even though she has now left this job. Our friendship seemed like a gift from the universe that only happened because we both followed the signs and our intuition. Often, unexpected events bring about new opportunities, new friendships or new relationships.

Staying open to the possibilities is important. Signs and synchronicities can pop up at any stage but they seem to occur more frequently when we are in the flow of source energy and in tune with our souls. Or maybe we just notice them more. It could be that a song keeps playing on the radio, or in our head, and it has a message for us. When I was going for a job many years ago, the song that kept playing included the words 'You go girl'. I knew I would get that job.

ANIMAL SIGNS

It could be that we keep seeing a certain animal. For me it is often the blue wren. He seems to appear when I am on the right track. Often it is an image of the wren but sometimes it is the actual bird. When I was looking for land to start a farm some years ago, I knew it was the right land to buy not only because it felt right but because I kept seeing blue wrens every time I visited the land.

Some signs will be actual signs or words that jump out at you or that repeatedly pop into your life. It may be a stop sign that you keep noticing, asking you to stop rushing so much. Or a sign on the side of a car or bus that has a particular message for you.

Sometimes, the synchronicity leads you to a new relationship or friendship. Sometimes, it leads you to a new job opportunity. Sometimes, it just reminds you of the wonder of the universe. Signs and synchronicities usually help you on your path.

I was recently struggling with the balance between GP work and writing. I had reached some clarity, through a series of synchronous events, that GP work was there for making enough money to fund my writing. I had worked out that writing can also be work but it just doesn't feel like it. I began to look at myself as a writer who also works in medicine rather than as a doctor who writes. I decided that if I focused on my writing then life would be much better. I asked for a sign about what direction I should take with work to make enough money to fund my writing. My current GP work just didn't seem viable.

I contacted a locum agency to see what my options were and a lovely woman called Angela rang me to discuss it. It was my friend Angela whose death started me on my writing journey so I took this as a good sign. There was a locum available at Halls Gap in the Grampians for four days a week from July to October that sounded like it was just what I needed to fund my writing. It also sounded like good work. I was torn between wanting to do it and feeling I still owed it to my patients to wait it out and see if the GP work was viable. I needed more signs to point me in the right direction. My gut feeling was I should close my practice and do locums but I wasn't completely sure. I felt guilty about leaving patients in the lurch again. I didn't like disappointing people.

I listened to a tarot reading and it said that I needed to change something major in my life, either my work or my relationship or my living situation. It said I had to give myself permission to change and not worry about other people but to put myself first. It said not to wait for a sign but to do what I needed to do before chaos descended on my life.

Then my fax machine and printer started to get glitchy, causing me problems at work and making it harder to do my job. One of our receptionists quit. I realised then that I needed to take some action and so I applied for the locum in Halls Gap. If I couldn't get it, I would stay at my practice to see if things improved. If I got the job, that would be a definite sign that I needed to move on. Of course, I got the job.

Everything is Connected

Signs and synchronicities are those weird moments when you feel like the universe is sending you a message. Or something happens that demonstrates everything is connected.

Recently, I went out for breakfast with an old friend. In the afternoon, I texted her to thank her and to tell her some other things. At exactly the same time, she was texting me. Our texts passed in the ether and hers arrived just as I sent mine.

The other day I had been thinking about my brother and wondering how he was when he rang to tell me he wasn't well. It is these weird synchronistic events that led me to believe there is a force in the universe that is always helping us along our path. If we pay attention to the signs and synchronicities, then we can follow our path more closely. Then, we tend to get more signs and synchronicities, or maybe it's just because we notice them when we're paying better attention.

Sometimes signs can be negative, letting us know we're not on the right path. My computer always acts up when I'm not following my path in writing. If the writing is forced or in some way not flowing, my computer will usually act up, letting me know to give it a rest.

If you're having trouble with technology, there is usually a message behind it.

WEB OF ENERGY

All of this sounds a bit crazy to a logical rational person but once you begin to tap into your own intuition and pay attention to signs and synchronicities, you begin to realise that everything is connected. These are energetic connections. You usually can't see them but they do exist, forming a giant web of energy within and around you so that what you do affects the web and the web is always affecting you. I don't exactly know how the web works but it has intelligence and this intelligence is what causes signs and synchronicities to occur. Cause is usually a linear way of thinking but in the energy web, the cause is never linear, it is nonlinear. Nonlinear causality is a completely different concept to linear causality and I don't understand how it works because it isn't logical. I just accept that it does work and that this energy intelligence is helping me on my path all the time if I pay attention.

TOOLS

PAYING ATTENTION

Sometimes, we sleepwalk through our lives and don't pay attention to all the miracles that surround us. Once we wake up to the energies of the universe, we find it easier to pay attention. Signs and synchronicities are all around us and as we notice them more, it seems that they happen more often. Some signs point us in the right direction while others, which may be perceived as negative, show us that we're stuck in some way or headed in the wrong direction. Everything that happens to us that makes us sit up and take notice is a sign that helps us discover our path. The missed flight, the car breakdown, the illness or the accident. If we pay attention to everything that happens to us, we begin to see that everything is connected and whatever happens to us brings us closer to our true path.

WRITE IT DOWN
Stories of signs and synchronicities often bring smiles to our faces as we recognise the interconnectedness of everything in our lives. Writing down our stories helps us see that whatever happens will help us transform our life into something better. Journalling is a wonderful daily practice that helps us reflect on what is happening. We may not recognise a sign or a synchronicity until we write about it and then we see its significance. The more we recognise these things in our life, the more they seem to happen and our whole life becomes a series of mini miracles.

CHAPTER 6

Looking After Our Physical Body

THE BODY IS THE PHYSICAL house of the soul and spirit and in the holistic worldview, everything is connected to everything else in one giant web. If we neglect our physical self we are also neglecting our spiritual self. If we neglect our spiritual side it can end up in physical ailments, and neglecting our physical body can show up in physical or spiritual dis-ease. We can't separate the two parts of our being. The whole of our being is energetic, so the energy of our physical body is important and it influences the other layers of our energy field.

How do we best look after our physical body? There are three main areas that we can look at in relation to the physical body:

- Diet
- Exercise
- Sleep.

Each of us is unique and has different dietary preferences and requirements but most of us will be healthiest if we follow a good diet. Dietary guidelines in the western world have until recently reflected the thinking that saturated fat is bad for us and carbohydrates are better. This way of thinking has led to an epidemic of obesity, diabetes and chronic disease. It is now known that sugar, simple carbohydrates and processed food have negative health consequences.

What Constitutes a Good Diet?
Our food should be fresh, minimally processed and as natural as possible.

If it is heavily processed and contains chemicals and artificial preservatives, sweeteners, sugar or fructose, it probably isn't good for us.

The foods that are good for us include firstly vegetables, preferably organic. That much is generally agreed upon; eat plenty of vegetables. But then what? Should we eat meat? Dairy? Grains? Or should we avoid some of these foods? How much fruit do we need?

I have put on weight since menopause and have found that the only way to shed it and keep it off is to eat mainly vegetables with some meat, fish, eggs and nuts. I try to avoid milk but do eat some cheese and yoghurt. I have practically cut out alcohol and have no sugar and minimal refined carbohydrates. This ketogenic type diet works for me and is sustainable. I can have the occasional day when I eat carbohydrates or have a glass of wine. But everyone is different and has to work out what way of eating is best for them as an individual, making sure it is sustainable in the long term.

I believe we should try to eat organic food and naturally raised meat, fish, dairy and eggs if we eat these products. Organic food has been shown to be better for us. The fewer pesticides and hormones we ingest through food, the healthier we will be.

I also believe we should eat as naturally as possible and therefore avoid processed foods and artificial sweeteners, colours or preservatives. There are certain foods we should all avoid. Sugar is the most important of these. It is addictive and it puts our pancreas under stress. It leads to weight issues and chronic diseases. Sugar is added to many processed foods, which is one of the reasons it is good to cut these out of the diet. Avoid soft drinks, fruit juices, lollies, cakes, etc. For better health and to prevent weight problems, it is best to also avoid simple refined carbohydrates such as bread, pasta, rice and the like, which all metabolise into sugars in the body. Alcoholic drinks often contain sugar or are metabolised into sugars.

Overall dietary guidelines are tricky and I believe we need to decide as individuals what we are going to eat. Most of us have a good idea of what we should be eating to be healthier, yet many of us don't do it. We end up eating the cake instead of the fruit, the pasta instead of the vegetables, drinking the wine instead of the water. What is it within us that sabotages our efforts to live a physically healthy life?

Again, this is an individual thing. Some of us eat for comfort when we are lonely or bored or anxious or depressed. Some of us turn to the glass of wine or the sugary snack after a stressful day. Some of us have fallen into habits of buying takeaway when we are busy or stressed. We allow the stress and busyness of our lives to dictate our eating habits instead of putting ourselves first.

To be healthy, we have to put ourselves first and make health a priority. If we aren't willing to do this then we should not feel guilty. For some people, other things are a priority but for me, looking after my physical body is one way to be true to my inner self. In order to manifest my soul and spirit externally, I need to be healthy of body. This takes effort and discipline.

When I look at the reasons for not always looking after myself properly it is usually because I am not putting myself first. I am doing something that other people want me to do that isn't in my best interests. I have become too busy and don't have time to look after myself. The antidote to this is to pare my life back to what is necessary. I cover this more in later chapters. For now, it is important to examine what is stopping us from being at our healthiest. What are the reasons behind eating too much of the wrong foods and not doing enough activity? We must let our body and intuition guide us to the answers.

EXERCISE

We all know that exercise is good for us. Picking activities that suit us individually is important, and paying attention to our bodies all the time helps us refine what is best for us. For me, walking, swimming, yoga, tai chi and gardening are great activities. My body doesn't like running or endurance activities; it lets me know pretty quickly that I'm not suited to such things.

Paying attention to what makes us feel good and what activities lead to injuries or pain is a good way to let our bodies lead us to the best activities as individuals. Obviously, stiff muscles after any new exercise is likely but ongoing pain or discomfort may be telling us to reconsider the activity.

The main thing about exercise and activity is to do some every day.

SLEEP

Sleep is the third aspect of a healthy lifestyle. It is essential for our health, for healing and restoration. Research shows that adults require between eight and eight and a half hours every night for good restorative sleep, and the optimum hours are between 9 pm and 5 am. Delta wave sleep, which is the best restorative sleep, has been shown to occur mainly between 9 pm and 2 am. Restorative and healing hormones are produced during this time. Poor sleep patterns over the long term lead to an increased risk of degenerative diseases such as obesity, diabetes and cardiovascular disease.

I have written about how to establish a good sleep pattern on my website so I won't repeat it here. I will just emphasise that good sleep is a very important part of a healthy lifestyle and we should again put our needs first and prioritise a good night's sleep over other less important things.

CHAPTER 7

Relationships and Connections

ONE OF THE GREATEST ILLUSIONS we adhere to is that we are separate from everything else. Of course we appear to be separate, but we are not really separate. We are connected to the rest of the system in many ways. Some of the connections are obvious, some of them are mysterious.

This chapter is about our connections with everyone else and how we can choose to either be connected and in harmony with the rest of the system or be disconnected and not in harmony. To be aware that we have this choice, we must first be aware that the connections are possible and that connecting increases our harmony within the system and our happiness and health.

Health and happiness is about nurturing our connections with the people, things and systems that increase our health and happiness.

Specifically, I want to look at our relationships with other people.

In a relationship between two people, there are not only the two people but the relationship itself. The relationship is the connection between the two people, the energy that flows between and around them.

The relationship changes as each person changes. In all relationships, there is a constant ebb and flow as the people within them move. The movement is like a dance. We move together and apart, seeking both intimacy and separation.

The lessons we are to learn are our lessons, not the other person's. If I want something to change in a relationship, it is entirely up to me. I have the power to change myself, which will change the relationship (although I am never quite certain how it will change the relationship).

We all fall into patterns of behaviour (habits) that don't always work for us. These patterns don't work because usually, we are living from a part of our ego rather than from our soul. The patterns lead us to make the same mistakes over and over until we learn about them and seek to change ourselves. Then we gain an increasing awareness of the patterns we get sucked into, which usually began in our childhood. We tend to replay the same pattern indefinitely until we realise we can do something different.

In all our relationships, we are tempted to believe that it is the other person who needs to change. Be it an intimate relationship, a friendship or even a relationship where we don't particularly like the other person, we want to lay the faults of the relationship at the other person's feet. We want them to take responsibility and we want them to make it right.

What our inner self wants is growth and change. Our soul puts us in relationships that are hard and messy so we can learn more about ourselves. When we get sick, we would really like someone else to fix us. When we have difficult interactions with another person, we would really like them to fix it. We all shy away from the work of our own souls and hope that someone else will save us.

But this isn't going to happen. We need to take responsibility for what we bring to any relationship, to any interaction with another person. This is the path of the soul, the journey to wholeness. Relationships continually challenge us to follow our path. They challenge us to transform our relationships through transforming ourselves. They challenge us to manifest our true selves in all our relationships.

SHADOWS

Each person is a complex system of interconnecting parts. Each part has light and dark, like the yin-yang symbol. In light there is also dark and in dark there is also light. All of us are tempted to align ourselves with one of these – we believe we are either light or dark, we believe we are either good or bad, honest or dishonest, loyal or disloyal, loving or hating, giving or taking.

Yet each of us is both good and bad, honest and dishonest, beautiful and ugly, happy and sad, rich and poor, sexually provocative and sexually innocent. Our shadow is the side of us we try to disown or suppress because we believe that we shouldn't have it.

All of us have the shadow and the shadow is not bad; it is a part of who we are. It causes us problems when we refuse to acknowledge it as part of us. Mostly this is an unconscious or subconscious thing – we actually convince ourselves that we don't have a shadow. But it always comes to visit and it usually comes in the form of another person.

When we disown a part of ourselves, we are then irresistibly drawn towards people who display this part. So it is said that opposites attract. We attract into our lives those people who display the parts of ourselves that we have tried to disown or suppress.

We seek always to move towards wholeness and this wholeness involves balancing the two sides of every aspect. If we have too much yin, we draw the yang towards us. If we have too much yang, we attract the yin.

Our lesson is to pay attention to the other person in the relationship but to change something in ourselves. The change may be about acknowledging the parts of ourselves that we have disowned or concealed. It may be about letting go of old patterns of behaviour that are no longer useful. It may be about learning new ways of loving others.

How do we start to look at relationships differently, as simply more opportunities to learn about ourselves?

There are two major ways we use to avoid our shadows. The first is mirroring and the second is projecting.

MIRRORING/REFLECTIONS

What we see in another person is a reflection of ourselves, a mirror that shows us our own lessons.

I thought one of my daughters was stubborn and headstrong and we often used to clash. For years, I wondered why she was like that. I thought about what I could do to get her to change. Then I started to wonder what she might be trying to teach me. How was I being stubborn and headstrong in my interactions with her? When I got frustrated that she wouldn't listen to me, I had to wonder in what ways I wasn't listening to her. When she got angry and yelled, I began to wonder whether I was handling my anger towards her behaviour poorly. She is still teaching me.

Some time ago, we went out to lunch after an orthodontist appointment. Something had gone wrong. She had got the wrong colour bands on her braces and she was upset with me. We sat at the table waiting for our order. She was aloof and not talking. I felt angry and tried to draw her out and sort out her anger. Nothing worked and I just got more and more frustrated. Then I wondered what was really going on here. It was a battle of two egos, each trying to gain control.

So I paid attention to how I was feeling – mainly angry and frustrated. I let the anger just simmer away without speaking. Then I wondered why I couldn't get her to see reason on this, why she wouldn't listen to me. Then, I had to turn it around and wonder how I was not listening to her. I realised that I hadn't listened to her complaint about the wrong colour bands. I had just said, 'That doesn't matter,' and dismissed it.

By then, my anger had had its turn and I was starting to feel sorry that I hadn't listened. I could also see that I had been fixed on a particular outcome. I wanted her to stop being grumpy with me, for everything to be 'nice' between us. In a way I had been trying to stop her feeling whatever it was she was feeling and get her to be happy so we could have a nice lunch. I had been trying to get her to put on a happy face, to pretend nothing was wrong so I could enjoy my lunch. I was expecting her to cover up her feelings so that I would not feel uncomfortable.

Within a few minutes I was able to let go of this outcome. I decided I could still have a nice lunch by myself, that I didn't have to punish her emotionally for feeling grumpy or angry. My heart seemed to expand then and I felt more loving. Suddenly it didn't matter whether she talked to me or not.

I told her I was sorry for not listening to her about the braces but that now, I couldn't do anything about it until we saw the orthodontist again. And then I just sat and ate my lunch. Then we started talking about how we get angry with each other and how funny we are sometimes when we get like that. She finished her lunch and wanted to go to the shop nearby while I finished mine. Now that I had let go of my outcome of wanting a nice lunch with her I didn't mind that she wanted to go shopping.

Within a short space of time I had moved from a position of being firmly entrenched in my ego, doing battle with my daughter's ego, to a completely different position. It was all to do with an internal shift away from ego towards soul. I had paid attention to how I was feeling and tried to view her reactions as a mirror of my own. I had stopped trying to reach an outcome that needed her to change and instead, looked at how I might change.

The beauty of the whole interaction and my newfound ability to shift away from my fixed outcome transformed the process. Once I stopped trying to get her to behave in a certain way (to stop being grumpy and be nice to me), the interaction changed and miraculously, both our behaviours changed.

The awareness of this mirroring effect helps us to work out what qualities are being reflected back to us in any interaction and sort out how we might change our behaviour. We can begin to imagine in what ways the other person's annoying behaviour is really just a reflection of our own.

The flip side of all this is that when we see love and beauty and joy in other people, this is also a reflection of ourselves. What we see around us is like a mirror. As we become channels for the spirit of love and we centre our lives around our souls, we see the same thing reflected back to us. In this way, we can monitor our movement towards wholeness by the mirror of our own world.

PROJECTION

Projection is a subconscious defence mechanism we all use to avoid some of our own stuff by projecting it onto another person. This lets us pretend it isn't our stuff but someone else's. We are not consciously aware of doing it.

We disown parts of ourselves because we have been taught to do so. For example, many of us believe that we shouldn't be greedy so we try to lose this part of ourselves. We push our greed down, suppress it, and send it into our subconscious. When it rises up, we tell ourselves we shouldn't feel greed and we manage to convince ourselves that we are not greedy. Yet greed is just the other half of generosity. We are all a balance between being partly generous and partly greedy.

In disowning our greedy self, we then project it onto other people (or sometimes other things). When this happens in a relationship, we find ourselves becoming polarised over the issues. One person takes on the greedy part and one the generous and both try to disown the other aspect.

This can occur with any quality of opposites that exists – good and bad, logical and illogical, emotional and unemotional. The list goes on forever. What we disown in ourselves we project out into the world so that we can see it. We get stuck when we continue to believe that it is the world and everyone else around us who need to change rather than ourselves. As we begin to own those discarded parts of ourselves, we stop finding them so annoying in other people.

In one relationship I was in, I found myself becoming more and more frustrated at my partner's logical approach to everything. We would discover an issue between us and he would take the analytical, logical approach and try to dissect the problem. I on the other hand would take the intuitive, feeling approach and get angry with him for not going with his feelings or acting on his intuition. Over time, we became a pair of opposites – he, the typical logical male and me, the typical intuitive female (read weepy and emotional!). The more I got in touch with my feelings, the more logical he became and the more logical he became, the more upset I became.

I don't know about him but I gradually realised I was projecting all my logical stuff onto him. Here I was writing a book about weird stuff; moving from a logical scientific viewpoint to an intuitive, holistic, metaphysical viewpoint. I was struggling with the side of myself that had been in charge for so long – the masculine side, the logical physically-based doctor side. In a sense I was trying to shed that part of me but in the process, I was trying to completely disown it. So I ended up projecting it onto my partner and denying its existence in myself.

He, in turn, was probably projecting his intuitive side onto me so we ended up putting all the stuff we didn't want onto the other person. No wonder we began to think the other person was some kind of enemy.

In this way, some of our most intimate relationships can turn sour because we won't own our own stuff. I realised that moving to a new worldview didn't mean I had to get rid of my logical side. It meant I needed to integrate it with my intuitive side. I needed to own that part of me that in some respects I saw as the enemy.

We do this projection all the time with other cultures when we don't want to own some parts of ourselves, projecting the notion of evil onto another country or group of people so we can pretend that it doesn't exist in us. Or we label a group of people as emotional and feel that we are acting from a higher logical viewpoint.

Mirroring and projecting are similar processes.

In mirroring, we see in other people what we need to see in ourselves.

In projection, what we see in another are those parts of ourselves that we are having trouble connecting to because we have disowned them. It is similar to mirroring except that we actually put our stuff onto the other person and then we judge them for being wrong in some way.

The two processes occur at the same time.

In order to use this knowledge about mirroring and projection, we need to ask ourselves some questions in any interaction.

- What is being reflected back here?
- What might I be projecting onto this person that I don't want to own?
- What do I see in this person that I can't see in myself?

Tools

I have two guidelines for transforming all our relationships so they give our souls more opportunity to grow. While it is a simplistic view, it always helps me when I'm stuck or when there are problems in a relationship.

Stop Trying to Change the Other Person's Behaviour

It is useful to stop believing that you know the other person better than they know themselves. It may help to stop thinking you are right and they are wrong and if only they could see things as you do, and change, everything would be all right.

One of the things we are learning about in relationships is love. We are learning to love ourselves, to love the other person and to be loved by the other. It gets tricky because we are learning all these things at the same time.

We try to love others for who they are, not for how they behave. This is unconditional love, this is what we all could practise (practise means trying to do it, always learning how to do it a little better). Try to forgive them for their human weaknesses. Choose to show your love for them in ways that they understand.

This does not mean we have to put up with behaviour that we don't like. It just means we should stop making it our job to change our friends, partners, children and people we don't even know very well. If we are in close relationships with people, part of our responsibility to the relationship might be to tell the person we don't like some of their behaviour. Then, having told them, we don't need to become responsible for their change. We need to learn to trust the process of their lives just as we are learning to trust the process of our own.

Their personal change and transformation is their job. Let it be their job, leave it to them, and don't get involved in stuff that is their stuff. Other people are responsible for their own lives and their own behaviour. When we take over this responsibility, we are saying two things to them: there is something wrong with them, and we are going to fix it. Thus, we take the responsibility away from them. We feel more powerful and they often feel less powerful.

None of this means that the person we are in relationship with does not need to change. Change is a prerequisite for growth. It simply means it is not our responsibility to try to change them. It is their choice to change or not.

One of the problems we encounter as we progress along our soul's path is that we become aware of people who are so entrenched in ego-centred living that they are unable to change, or the change is so slow that we can't stand to watch. It is easier with people we have a superficial relationship with but much harder when it is those who are close to us. Yet we cannot know what it is they are learning or how they are to learn it. They are teaching us patience and tolerance and any number of things as they go through their process.

All we can do is learn our own lessons and leave everyone else to learn theirs.

START TRYING TO CHANGE YOUR OWN BEHAVIOUR

This is about bringing your behaviour in line with your inner self. Listen to the messages from your soul and pay attention. The most common message from your soul is that which is reflected back to you from the other person. The person you are having a relationship with, be it friend, partner, child or parent is always a mirror.

The difficulties in all our relationships are in fact opportunities to learn more about ourselves and how we might change for the better. Near the end of my marriage, the things that concerned me about my then-husband were also the things that I needed to change in myself. He didn't listen to me. He didn't understand me. He wouldn't talk about how he really felt.

At the time I thought it was mostly his problem but with some distance, I could see that I wasn't listening to him, or even to myself half the time. I didn't understand him and I certainly didn't understand myself. I had trouble talking about how I really felt. While he may have had all those problems too, what I didn't realise back then was that while I had no power or control over his behaviour, I did over my own.

I could have chosen to listen to him, to try to understand him and talk about how I really felt. It would have changed the outcome in many ways if I had been open enough to do something different, instead of always wanting him to do the something different. At the time, I thought I was doing something different and maybe I was, but the biggest mistake I made was believing that if only he would change things would be different. I needed to change that belief to 'if only I changed, things would be different', because they would have been.

CHAPTER 8
Finding Joy and Passion

WHAT LIGHTS YOU UP? How do you find joy? Are you living your passions?

There are different ways of saying it but what they all have in common is the feeling we get when we are doing something authentic. It comes from within and nurtures our soul and opens our heart to the flow of the universe. When we find what lights us up or brings us joy or fills us with passion, we know we are in flow with source energy. It flows through us and we shine our authentic light on the world.

Yet too often we don't pay enough attention to what lights us up or brings us joy. We don't always believe we are allowed to live like that. We don't believe we are allowed to live a life full of joy. Yet this is the path to follow in being authentic. The things that bring us joy highlight the way of the soul. When we follow the moments of joy and passion, we discover the path of a soulful life.

This is how we are meant to live, moment by moment reaching for the things that light us up from the inside. This is how we look after ourselves and fill ourselves with light that can shine on others and help them.

For too long, I had been doing things for other people and not taking the time to look after myself. When I began to follow the path of joy-filled moments, I discovered that I could finally look after myself and my soul. It may not be as simple as just following joy but sometimes, living a spirit-filled, authentic life is as simple as following our passions and doing those things that light us up.

What lights me up and fills me with joy?

- Writing
- Gardening, plants and flowers
- Tarot reading
- Crystals
- Beeswax candles
- Connecting with people on an authentic level
- Using my intuition and logic together
- Walking on the beach
- Helping people discover their soul answers
- Knitting
- Caring for the land
- Reading

What brings you joy and lights up your life? Think about it, and then do more of these things. You will find your soul's path much easier to follow. This is the way to lead an authentic life.

It is possibly as simple as this, but we have become so entrenched in society and its cultural values that we have to keep reminding ourselves. Do more of what you love. Follow your passions.

We know deep inside us how to live a soul-led life but we have forgotten, so it often takes many steps to get there. We need to pay more attention, to our feelings, our bodies and our intuition. We need to let go of outcomes. We need to follow the process. We need to remember all our lessons. This may be the biggest and most important lesson because it connects us directly to our soul's path.

Do what you love. Do what lights you up. Do what brings you joy. And don't apologise for doing this.

Don't believe that you are being selfish. You have unique gifts to bring to the world and you cannot bring them if you are not living from soul. Nor can you live from soul unless you follow your passions.

You must take care of yourself first.

You must put your need for authenticity ahead of everything else.

I was going to write more extensively here about the difference between what lights us up and what gives us short-term gratification, such as an addiction or the temporary satisfaction we feel when coming from a place of ego. But I think we can all tell when something genuinely lights us up and fills us with joy, compared to short-term gratification or temporary satisfaction. When something lights us up, when we find joy in an activity or pursuit, when we are passionate about something, then we light up from the inside out. We channel spirit through our soul centre and it flows out into the world. We can identify this as being in the flow and it is quite different from the feeling of doing something from a position of ego to try to feel good.

We all know this feeling. The things that light us up help us to channel spirit and become soul centred.

This centring of our whole life around the needs of our soul is what we have come here to do. To lead a soul-centred life is to bring our gifts to the world in a way that only we can. It is not selfish to centre our lives around the needs of our soul. It is the only way to live an authentic life and bring the light of spirit into the world. Our joy spreads into the world. Our light becomes the light of the world. Our passion inspires others to follow their passions. We fill ourselves with love and then we can help other people do the same. We are all connected, so being soul centred and a channel for light and love means that we can change the world.

We can move from a fear-based culture to a love-based culture. All it takes is for each one of us to follow the path of joy. Fill your life with joy and light and you will become a channel for spirit to work through you. You will be an instrument of source energy and the divine, which is what we have come here to be.

As mentioned earlier in the book, in my work journey, I only recently realised that what lights me up most is my writing. I had been searching for some type of GP work that lit me up but I just kept moving from one job to another, never finding any clinical work that really lit me up or brought me much joy. Eventually, I realised that my paid work is just there to fund my writing, which is what really lights me up and brings me joy. I was finally able to view my paid work as a means to write and I could stop looking for something in that work that brought me joy in the way writing does.

I had been constantly dissatisfied with my GP work but once I realised it had the purpose of helping me write, I was able to view it differently. My aim was to eventually earn money from writing but for now, I could see the GP work had a purpose. I stopped trying to turn it into something it wasn't and became much happier about doing it.

I decided I had to really become disciplined about doing the writing or otherwise I was wasting my time. So I began getting up early every morning before work to spend at least an hour writing. Each day I would start with this joyful activity and this helped me be more present during the day for my patients. I was doing more of what I was passionate about at the very start of the day and it helped me bring some of that light to my GP work. It also made me see that I had been putting too much pressure on myself in trying to find joy in the GP work; it could never match the joy I found in writing. But there were moments of joy in helping people and when I started the day in flow, I found more of these moments.

If, then, finding joy in life is as simple as following joyful moments and doing what lights us up, why am I writing more about ways to transform our life?

As we become awakened and aware, we often struggle to stay in the space of flow. We move in flow for some of the time but then forget to do the joyful things and get stuck. Much of what I write about in this book is ways to get unstuck. After all, life and becoming authentic is a process. Transforming ourselves into channels for source energy is a process. We are still human and have learnt human ways and culture. Most of us cannot step straight into being channels of light and love all the time. Sometimes we need other ways to help us navigate life and that is where the other strategies in this book will help.

TOOLS

BOOKS

The following three books are among my favourite because they explore how we can follow our passions and live lives that are soulful and magical.

Big Magic: Creative Living Beyond Fear – Elizabeth Gilbert. Bloomsbury Paperbacks, 2016.

The Soul's Code: In Search of Character and Calling – James Hillman. Bantam UK, 1997.

Care of the Soul – Thomas Moore. Piatkus, 2012.

COACHES

If you're having trouble with finding purpose and direction, look for a coach who can help you discover more about your passions and the best ways to follow your path of joy. Sometimes we get stuck and need someone else to push us along and help us discover our path. A coach could be a friend or family member who is willing to sit and listen and provide feedback. It could be a counsellor or psychologist who helps you gain clarity about what direction you want to go. Or it could be a life coach or someone who is specific to an area of interest such as a writing coach or a business coach. Again, use your intuition, follow word-of-mouth recommendations and pay attention to signs in order to find the right person. Just be aware of not trying to hand over responsibility to them; you've still got to do the work.

WRITE IT OUT

Using a journal is a great way to help you find your passion and joy in life. I keep a daily journal and always write about what things have brought me joy. Writing itself is a joy for me but even if you find it hard to keep a journal, I encourage you to try it for a month. Write about how you feel and what brings you the most joy. Keep track of signs from the universe. Be grateful for all your experiences and create a space where you can reflect on what your experiences are teaching you.

CHAPTER 9
Connecting With the Earth

BECOMING AWARE AND SOUL CENTRED connects us with our inner self. For some of us, it feels like a homecoming. We can stop searching for answers outside of ourselves and find the answers within. The answers are in that place of soul where we connect with the divine and source energy. Yet we are still human and ultimately being on earth in this life shapes our experience.

Some time ago I was living a very light-filled life. I was in flow and full of joy and light. But I forgot to stay connected to the earth. I forgot I was human and needed to be grounded. So I floated away. I saw the whole world as energy, a field of shimmering light and colour. And it was too much for some part of my human self to take. I lost myself for a while and ended up having what is called a puff of madness, a short-term psychosis. I lost touch with reality for a few days.

This happened twice in a couple of years and I am currently writing a book based on the experience which I hope to publish in 2021. For many years after, I was too scared to fully explore the world of spirit again. I made sure I was grounded in human reality. I feared if I channelled spirit fully I would go crazy again. So I contracted my energy and anchored myself to the earth. This was very healing and I learnt a lot about the earth and her energy. My soul was healing from the shock of too much energy flowing in my upper chakras without the grounding of the lower ones. I learnt once again that I am not just my thoughts, for they disappeared for a short time. It seemed that I was all right brain and my left brain logic had left. But it was also as if my very soul had left. It may have been my imagination (or my craziness) but my soul seemed to leave my body and expand out. I saw the world in a completely different way. If I had been in a different culture, these episodes might have been treated differently and instead of medication I would have been taught how to channel the information I received. It has taken me nearly ten years to be able to write about it and see my lessons.

Stay grounded. Stay connected to the earth. Be like a tree. Complete the circle.

I'm not saying you'll go crazy if you aren't grounded and connected to the earth but for me, it is very important to connect to the energy of the earth. The circle of life includes both heaven and earth and our bodies are the conduits for the energy that flows around and through us. Like the tree on the cover with its roots in the earth and its leaves in the sky, the energy flows through and around us like a sphere. We channel the energy of both heaven and earth and bring together the masculine and feminine energies. In this way, we become whole beings and inhabit both the physical and spiritual dimensions.

I want to emphasise that connecting to earth is not just about grounding, which is anchoring ourselves to physical reality. It is also about channelling the earth energy up through our body. At the same time, we can channel the energy from the heavens downwards. These energies meet in the heart, which is where the soul lives. And this is what lights up our soul best. When the feminine energy of the earth meets the masculine energy of the sky, we move into flow. The physical and spiritual realms are united. I know this sounds a bit poetic and difficult to visualise but when we experience this union of heaven and earth, we come to see the world differently. We awaken to what is beyond the physical but we are still anchored in the physical by our connection to earth.

We are akin to the plants that have their roots deep in the dark soil where they get nourishment and water. The visible part of the plant reaches to the sun but if it doesn't have its roots deep in the soil, it will topple and die. We must anchor ourselves to the earth or we become top-heavy and we too topple over. The earth is our base, she is the mother. As we channel spirit through us from the earth, we can bring about healing for ourselves and the earth. This is our home in the present life.

Spirit exists in all places; it is not just above us. We might open our crown chakra to receive universal energy, but we can also receive it from the earth via our base chakra. Energy flow is not just a vertical line but a circuit, and it flows in all directions. Imagine we are balls of light. As we channel energy, we enlarge and expand. It is this expansion that changes our world.

It may be hard to picture what is happening when we align ourselves with source energy. Some picture it as a cross where the energy pours in via the crown chakra and down into the earth while the horizontal element extends from the heart outwards. This is a limited view. If we view it as energy circulating through us and out around us like a sphere, we come closer to understanding. As we channel source energy, we expand our auric field and brighten it with white and gold light. However, our auric field needs grounding to the earth. If we begin to float away from the earth, we lose our foundation. Our foundation is the earth.

CONNECTING WITH THE EARTH

Sink your feet into the earth, feel your body sink into the earth, feel your body connecting with the earth energies.

Get your hands dirty in the garden, smell the darkness of the soil.

Walk on the beach or the grass barefoot.

Lie on the ground.

Embrace the tree as your friend and feel the energy of the earth seep into your bones.

If everything is one, then we are both heaven and earth. Yet sometimes we forget that we are earth because we are so much in our heads. We forget we have a lower half. We must nurture all of our energy centres and not believe that we are better for inhabiting our upper chakras. We do not become beings of light and love by forgetting we are human or forgetting that we should be deeply connected to the earth.

My lessons on grounding and connecting to the earth are personal lessons, but I believe it is important for everyone to be more balanced in their energy fields. It is like returning to the ancient wisdom of many indigenous cultures, which are in tune with the earth and embrace her spirit. The earth is a living being that supports our existence but she is more than that; she is part of us and we are part of her.

When I floated off into the ether, I had forgotten that I was still human. I was carried away by higher energies. I needed to reconnect with the grounding earth energies to help centre myself.

Indigenous cultures have a firm connection to the land and to the plants and animals. We can learn from them in many ways and one of them is learning about their connection to the earth.

Tools

Books

Braiding Sweetgrass – Robin Wall Kimmerer. Audiobook, 2015. I loved Robin's narration on audiobook. It's a wonderful mixture of scientific knowledge and indigenous wisdom about what plants have to teach us.

The Secret Teachings of Plants and *Sacred Plant Medicine* – both by Stephen Harrod Buhner, Inner Traditions Bear and Company, 2004 and 2006. These books are also based upon indigenous knowledge and look at the relationships people can have with plants and how plants communicate with people.

The Secret Network of Nature: The Delicate Balance of All Living Things – Peter Wohlleben. Penguin Random House UK, 2017. Looks at the intricate connections within systems and what happens when the systems get out of balance.

Get Outside

It's easy to connect with the earth; we just have to get outside. Even in big cities there are usually parks and gardens. Walk among the plants, walk barefoot on the earth or grass, meditate on a park bench among the greenery or just sit. Just sitting in nature is calming; it calms our sympathetic nervous system, which is often running on high from the frenetic pace of life. Take time out to spend time in nature and go to wild places when you can. If you're like me and live near the ocean, you can appreciate the wildness of the sea every day. Or if you live near bush or forest you can go out and feel the energies of the trees and rocks. These energies will help recharge you and connect you with spirit.

The energy of the earth can be hard to access from a high-rise building or in the middle of a concrete jungle so if you live in a place like that, spending time outdoors is even more important. Make time to connect with the earth regularly and you will find that her energy just seeps into you. Her spirit will calm your nerves and bring more joy to your life.

I love to appreciate her gifts that continually flow; the beauty of the crescent moon in the early morning sky, or the full moon as it rises, or the sunrises and sunsets that are all different, or a rainbow in a storm, or the storm itself, or the stars at night. All of these can be appreciated anywhere if you take time to go outside and look.

BUY A PLANT

Wherever you live you can bring some earth energies into your home by buying a plant. Some plants are fussy but there are many that do well indoors. Looking after them and paying attention to their needs connects you with earth energy. Plants help clear the air and bring life into a room.

My daughters have become plant addicts and spend much of their time and money sourcing plants for their homes. Their rooms are filled with plants and their houses are like plant nurseries. They have learnt to care for a variety of plants and pay attention to their needs and their moods. Too much water, too little sunshine, too much heat. Plants are living beings and cohabiting with them requires us to pay attention to their energy and their needs. It connects us with nature on an intimate level and nourishes our need to be connected to the earth.

You can bring earth energy into your home in other ways such as crystals or rocks, flowers, shells, driftwood, wooden furniture, fruit in a bowl. Having a home decorated with natural objects rather than plastics and artificial things brings the energy of the earth inside and enriches your life.

GROW YOUR OWN FOOD

Eating food is an obvious connection to mother earth because she provides it all. When we take the next step and grow some of our own food, we begin to appreciate the wonder of plants. The miracle of watching a seed turn into a seedling and flowers turn into fruit never fails to delight me. I watch the bare earth turn into rows of small pea sprouts and the sprouts send up stems with tiny tendrils that attach to anything they find. In weeks, they are flowering and tiny pea pods begin to appear. I notice the fruit tree is full of blossom and then before I know it, tiny fruits appear which grow and swell with the passage of days until they're ready to eat. I love the way zucchini plants always manage to hide some of their babies and suddenly I have monster zucchinis 30cm long. I love the smell of the mint leaves as I pick them for my tea and the spring smell of the daffodils that I plant for their sheer exuberance. My garden is a constant wonder.

Growing our own food not only brings many delights but it teaches us about the miracle of life and the certainty of death; the cycle of life in a garden is constant. We also bear closer witness to the cycle of the seasons and pay attention to the cycles of the moon. These things all bring us closer to the earth and enhance our appreciation of her many gifts.

Growing food is a wonderful way to enrich our lives. Even if you only have a small herb garden on a balcony or windowsill you will understand what I mean. Looking after plants is a rich part of our heritage as humans and eating the produce is the only way we have survived. Transforming our spaces into areas that provide our own food transforms our relationship with the natural world. It grounds us to the earth and connects us to the healing energy of plants.

Part Two

Transformative Practices

Transforming into a more soulful person is not only about paying attention to our inner self but also about awakening to the power of spirit. As we focus on our soul's needs rather than our ego's needs, we open ourselves up to spirit and source energy. This process wakes us up to the oneness of the universe and the realisation that we are part of something much bigger than just our human self. We awaken to higher consciousness and become aware of a higher power. Depending upon our belief system, this might be source energy or God in some form or simply the universe. Whatever we believe, this power is universal and flows through us all, connecting us and allowing us to achieve our higher purposes.

Generally, awakening occurs when we are broken open by something that happens in our lives. It might be a tragedy such as the death of a loved one, or something beautiful such as the birth of a child or falling in love. Our heart breaks open quite suddenly; our soul opens up and spirit flows in. In these moments, we suddenly realise that there is more to this life than we had previously thought. This process can occur many times in our lives. Sometimes big events and sometimes small ones help to break us out of ego and into heart and soul space.

I was aware of the spiritual side of life from my teenage years but it wasn't until I was in my forties that a sudden breakdown in my marriage opened my heart and soul to a different way of living. Later, also in my forties, my good friend Angela died quite suddenly which again broke my heart open further. A short time later, a love affair that had truly opened me up to love suddenly ended and the process happened again. Each time, it was as though I needed some chaos to break me open and awaken to a higher energy. It was like going in a spiral and getting deeper into my soul's existence, or higher in spirit each time.

It was after all these experiences that I decided to look at ways of living soulfully and becoming more awake without having to do so through crises and chaos. I started to look at ways I could transform my life into soul-centred, spirit-filled awareness. What I cover in the following chapters are the ways I have found that help me continually transform into who I am meant to be; transforming into my authentic whole self.

CHAPTER 10
Minimalism/Letting Go

A COUPLE OF YEARS AGO I decided that in order to transform myself and my life, I should start with the easiest dimension – the physical. I thought this might be tinkering around the edges but at the same time, I knew that as we are holistic beings, transforming the physical side of our life would inevitably affect the spiritual side and the whole. It's good to start somewhere that's easy.

DECLUTTERING

I began with decluttering my house. I wasn't exactly becoming a minimalist but it made me aware of how much stuff I had. More clothes than I needed, more books than I needed to keep, more of everything than I needed. The clutter of stuff can be suffocating, while the getting rid of stuff was liberating, allowing more space in my life. I had to make a real effort not to refill it with more stuff.

While decluttering, I discovered that I was much more of a consumer than I had thought. I mistakenly believed that I was treading lightly on this earth but as I sorted through piles of stuff, I realised I was as guilty as everyone else of buying much more than I needed. Even as I got rid of stuff I found I kept buying more.

It is an addiction, this consumerism. Society teaches us that we should buy and consume, and so we do. Sometimes without questioning. Decluttering has made me question my impact on the earth. I have given away lots of stuff, and I am now also much more aware of how much I am tempted to buy.

The investigation of decluttering and minimalism approaches led me to books and YouTube videos about zero waste. I became even more aware of how much waste I was creating with my consuming lifestyle.

I tried the approach that dictates that if something didn't bring me joy or it wasn't necessary, then I didn't need it. I tried to get rid of more stuff and tried very hard not to succumb to buying more. But I went in circles sometimes and found myself shopping online for things I didn't need, or doing more Christmas shopping than I needed to.

I began to notice how much rubbish I was generating and tried to cut back on plastic packaging. It is everywhere and we are drowning in the stuff.

I became a little obsessed with decluttering and not buying plastic. I stocked up on cloth bags for buying produce. I tried to work out ways of buying meat with no packaging. I avoided supermarkets.

When I began the process of decluttering about a year ago, I didn't realise it would take me to such a different place. I thought it would help my spiritual transformation and it has, but what I didn't realise is that it would transform the way I looked at the physical.

I have always considered myself a bit green but when I took stock of my effect on the world, I discovered I just liked to think of myself as green. I wasn't really very green at all. Sure, I grew some of my own food and bought organic food but really, it was tokenistic. I wasn't trying very hard to make a difference. So gradually, I began to try harder.

What I found was that thinking harder about the effect I was having on the earth brought me closer to the earth itself. I became more grateful for her gifts. I found myself thanking the chooks for the eggs and the plants for their vegies. I thought twice before I bought a punnet of blueberries, knowing the plastic case they came in would have an impact, whereas if I bought cherries in my reusable cloth bag I could forgo the plastic container.

How does all this relate to transformation of self? I believe that our spiritual selves are more in tune with the earth than our ego selves. I believe that our ego selves are the culprits when it comes to over-consumption. Abundance for the ego self is quite different from abundance for our spiritual self. Ego self is concerned with what we have, not so much with what everyone else has, or doesn't have. Our spirit is part of the greater whole, so it is aware of how what we consume affects the greater whole. If we over-consume, then the earth will suffer and other people will suffer. The giant web connects us all, not just in a spiritual sense but on a physical level as well.

Letting Go of Busyness

Minimalism and letting go of the physical stuff is just one step. The next step is letting go of the busyness in our lives. We do too much, full stop. Mostly, we do too much of the stuff that doesn't bring us joy or fulfilment or help us achieve our higher purpose. We get so busy we forget who we really are and how to bring our authentic gifts to the world.

Letting go of busyness is hard because society reveres the busy person, yet it is an important step towards soul.

Let go of doing and spend more time being. Step out of the rat race and spend time in nature and contemplation and meditation. Do more of what brings you joy and less of what doesn't. Allow yourself to do more stuff that is just for you and just for the fun of it. Treat yourself kindly and start saying no to stuff you don't want to do.

So we let go of physical stuff. We let go of busy stuff.

Letting Go of Emotional and Mental Stuff

We also need to let go of emotional and mental stuff. We need to let go of our baggage and our blockages. This is a hard concept to write about because everyone has different baggage and wounds.

In this life, we may suffer emotional and mental trauma and carry the wounds and scars with us. But the soul can also carry the wounds and scars of past life traumas. These wounds can influence our behaviour and we are often unclear about why we are reacting in a certain way or why we are feeling certain emotions or thinking certain thoughts.

Past Wounds

One major event in my life was when Angela died and some time after that, I fell in love with her widowed husband. This was a time when my heart was open with grief at losing Angela and love for this man. But it didn't work out and I was left with a doubly broken heart. The three of swords in the tarot deck. A love triangle complicated by death and then rejection.

Tools for Transformation

I have carried this heaviness in my heart for years without knowing that it was also a soul wounding; that it had probably happened in numerous past lives, a type of karmic wound.

I asked a friend to help me with this. Together, we explored why I was holding onto this wound. I needed to understand why I couldn't clear my heart blockage and let go of past wounds. As we worked with the discomfort, I felt I needed to know more about the circumstances of the past wounds and what the karmic pattern was. It seemed to me that we have all been wounded in the past and we keep repeating this karmic pattern. We are all connected by both love and pain.

I worked with my dreams and intuition to gain some insights into the past. I have done past life regression before but I didn't feel the need to revisit every painful experience. It was enough to realise that the three of us had been linked before and that the cycle involved both love and heartbreak.

I decided to let go of the pain and break the cycle. I needed to forgive us all, including myself. I wrote a letter, not to send but seeking forgiveness of myself and forgiving both people involved for any pain they had caused me. I practised opening my heart to the pain until gradually it dissipated.

I also did a guided meditation that released my soul from the past hurt and helped sever the ties I had with these soulmates of mine. I wanted to be free of the pain of hurt so that I could open my heart more fully. I began to be more open-hearted in all my relationships.

My heart blockage is but one example of holding onto past hurts and emotions. If we explore these pains and deep feelings we can let them go and move on with less baggage.

So, minimalism and letting go isn't just letting go of the physical stuff that clutters our lives, but also letting go of all the other clutter. The busyness. The wounds from this life that we have held onto. The old wounds and cellular memories that we hold onto for lifetimes sometimes.

Everyone has different ways of letting stuff go. The challenge is giving ourselves time to work through some of these issues and being open to clearing stuff away. In this way, we can live more simply and with greater clarity about who we are, unhindered by too much stuff.

TOOLS
BOOKS

The Life-Changing Magic of Tidying Up: The Japanese Art of Decluttering and Organizing – Marie Kondo. Vermilion, 2015. This book is a classic but it only looks at decluttering and letting go of physical things, although this often leads to other changes as we declutter. A great book with which to start the minimalism journey. Marie also has a television series based upon her methods.

Essentialism: The Disciplined Pursuit of Less – Greg McKeown. Currency, 2014. I listened to this on audiobook and its message resonated with me. It's about paring back our lives to what is essential rather than filling them with stuff.

The Year of Less – Cait Flanders. Hay House, 2018. This book is a chronicle of living with less for a year. It describes the transformations that came about in the process.

Letting Go: The Pathway of Surrender – David R Hawkins. Veritas, 2013. This book provides practical strategies to let go of wounds and blockages that might be holding you back.

Start Small

Don't be afraid to start small in your journey to let go. Just begin with what feels right. I started with my clothes and books and gradually worked around to other areas of my life. I began to buy less and tried to let go of my consumerist tendencies. Now if I want to go shopping, I choose to buy plants instead of more stuff, healthy food instead of processed food, good-quality clothes instead of fashion items.

If you're having trouble letting go of stuff, reflect on why this is. If you're holding onto being busy, contemplate what you might be avoiding by having more space and time in your life. If you're having trouble letting go of grudges or feelings, give yourself permission to take more time to process the feelings.

Starting small helps by not putting so much pressure on ourselves. It's like the saying 'How do you eat an elephant? One bite at a time.' Take your time and tackle each step in the process.

Be Kind to Yourself

Above all, be kind to yourself. Take the time to process your feelings about letting go of stuff and activities and old emotional baggage. Try not to fill the voids that decluttering creates by buying more, doing more, eating more or drinking more wine. Allow yourself to have some voids in your life that don't need filling except with your own energy. As you empty your life of the things that don't really matter, you can fill it with things that do, like meaningful relationships, joyful experiences, creativity and passion, connection and spontaneity.

As my life becomes simpler, I am always tempted to find things to occupy my time that I don't really want to do. Recently, I agreed to do a locum job because I thought I should. Now I regret taking it on as I would rather have more free time to write and garden. So be careful about what you agree to take on. Use your intuition to work out if it's something you really want to do or you just think you should do. We all do too much of what we think we should do and not enough of what we really want to do.

Simplify your life.

CHAPTER 11

Reflection, Contemplation and Meditation

REFLECTING IS THE PROCESS OF analysing and looking at something that has happened in order to learn from it.

Contemplation is the process of looking at something thoughtfully for a long time.

REFLECTION AND CONTEMPLATION

Reflection and contemplation are part of transformation because they help us look at our lives in a way that enables us to work out what is happening and where we can choose to walk a different path. Sometimes when we are ill or in psychological distress or our lives are in chaos, we get so tied up in knots that we can't even think straight. Giving ourselves time to sit back, take deep breaths and reflect on our lives is enormously important. We can contemplate what is going on in our lives in a way that looks at the deeper meanings and what lies beyond.

Both reflection and contemplation involve using analytical as well as intuitive thinking to process events that have happened in our lives. We take an event and sit with it, pulling it apart, looking at the whole thing and at the parts in order to understand and learn from it.

Reflecting and contemplating can be hard: they make us take responsibility for our lives. When we are under stress, we often look for external things or people to blame. When we take time to reflect on what is happening, we always bring it back to ourselves. What is my part in this? What lessons do I have to learn from this experience? What can I do to make a difference to the situation?

Reflection and contemplation are about looking at the situation and finding some meaning in it. We might reflect upon our illness and look at the possible reasons it has happened and the changes we might make to address the root causes. We might reflect upon a work situation that is causing us stress and think about our part in the process and how we might change that to bring about healing. Or we might reflect upon a situation that is causing us emotional turmoil and decide we are being asked to change the situation or relationship.

Reflection and contemplation do not always have immediate answers. It is a process that involves both the left and right sides of the brain. We look at things in a logical way and an intuitive way. We break it down and we look at the whole picture simultaneously. We stop trying to blame someone or something for our problems and look inside for our answers. Source energy (spirit) and our inner self (soul) are intimately connected, so we can access this divine spirit by looking inside.

Sometimes, no matter how much we reflect on something, it may not make sense to us. We may not be able to get to the root cause or find a lesson or make sense of it in any logical way. This usually means we need to find a way to accept it and move on. Often, understanding will come later. We will suddenly see why an event occurred or an illness happened. Other times, things remain a mystery and we never really understand them.

It's important to spend time to reflect and contemplate. I carve out some time each day to do so. I begin with journalling, writing down what has happened over the past day and reflecting on what I have learnt and what issues have come up. Then I often go for a walk on the beach, which for me is a form of meditation. My mind can reflect on things and contemplate life, or be empty for a while so that my intuition can pop answers to a problem into my head.

The other thing I do of course is writing. When I write, I am writing more from soul and spirit rather than from a logical place. I can then reflect on what I have written, and things make greater sense to me. The logic comes in when I am trying to organise what I have written into a more coherent whole.

Some people paint or dance or sculpt or do any number of creative things. All of these can be a form of reflection. Maybe when we get out of our logical mind a little in order to create something, we give room for our intuition to show us what we need to know. We can reflect on both joyful processes and difficult challenges and sort out our lives in a more meaningful way. How can we bring more joy to our lives and how do we cope with the challenges? The answers very often come to us in contemplation of the issue. This is not to say that thinking logically about an issue will always help us. I believe we need to think both logically and intuitively to understand the issue properly. It is a combination of left and right brain thinking that helps us understand the process of our lives and where we might make changes.

Many people meditate and find this helps with their reflection and contemplation, but I think they are separate processes and that we should make a separate time for reflection.

Sometimes, it is good to talk things over with another person in order to reflect and come to a greater understanding. I undertake clinical supervision to reflect upon my clinical practice. This helps sometimes when things are not clear or I am stuck in some way. My supervisor helps me look at issues in a different way and connect with my feelings better. She helps me reflect on what has happened in a more structured and holistic way than I sometimes do on my own. I would encourage you to access a good psychologist or counsellor if you are particularly stuck or unable to process an issue. Soul and spirit usually find a way through these stuck times if you can just step back and pay attention to what is really going on, but talking to someone else may help things become clearer in your mind.

MEDITATION

Meditation is different from reflecting and contemplating. It is more about not connecting to thinking, about somehow disconnecting from the logical thinking part of the brain and being in a space that is separate from the ego mind.

Some people meditate by focusing on the breath or the physical body or a particular mantra. In each case there is disconnection of the conscious awareness from the thinking mind. The meditator becomes more of an observer of the thoughts than the thinker of the thoughts.

You can also use mindfulness practices, observing your thoughts without focusing on them. You look at the thoughts as separate from the inner self and just observe them flitting through the mind.

Meditation helps connect you to your inner self and spirit. By disconnecting from your logical thoughts in this way, you are more likely to have intuitive insights that may help you process issues and problems.

There is plenty of information available on meditation, including many phone apps with meditations you can follow. The most important thing with meditation is not how long you do it for but that you do it regularly. It helps with calming the mind, getting more in touch with soul and spirit and tapping into your intuition. It has physical health benefits too in that it can reduce the effects of stress and lower high blood pressure. The busier your life, the more you will benefit from a meditation practice to help bring calm and balance back.

There are so many different ways to meditate and it is important to try different techniques to find one or two that are right for you. Some people use visualisation to meditate, but because I'm not very good at visualising I find that technique very difficult. I like to focus on the breath or just watch the thoughts come and go. Most of all, I find walking meditation good where I bring myself out of my head and into my body, aware of each step and connection to the earth. It's easy to fall back into thinking, so it takes a conscious presence to keep bringing the awareness back to the bodily sensations and movement and out of the thinking mind.

I also like to meditate on a flower or a candle flame or some other object of beauty. I bring my awareness to the flower or the flickering flame and observe all its features. This is a form of mindfulness, just being connected to the flower and in that way letting go of the thinking mind.

All three techniques, reflection, contemplation and meditation, are very useful to help us let go of the dominance of our rational mind and tap into the intuitive mind and spirit. When we get really busy, we forget to take time out for these processes, which all help us bring more balance and calm into our lives.

TOOLS

BOOKS

Meditation. There are books on meditation, but I prefer apps or classes to get into a good practice.

Reflection and Contemplation. Reading any book gives you an opportunity to reflect and contemplate its messages, and there are many that provide daily pieces to reflect on. Books such as *Notes From the Universe* by Mike Dooley (Beyond Words Publishing, 2007), *Simple Soulful Sacred* by Megan Dalla Camina (Hay House, 2019) or *A Year of Miracles* by Marianne Williamson (HarperCollins, 2016).

APPS

There are plenty of great apps on phone and tablet that lead you through meditations and reflections. I like *1 Giant Mind: Learn Meditation* and *Calm: Meditation and Sleep* but there are plenty of others that offer great content. Some are free and others cost a small amount. Some people like to do the same meditation over and over; others like variety. Different apps offer different techniques and strategies.

CLASSES

Meditation classes are a great way to learn different styles of meditation and they also help to get you into a meditation routine. Some classes also offer reflection and contemplation time where the leader will discuss a topic and there is time to reflect and contemplate as well as meditate. Yoga usually incorporates some relaxation and meditation and is a great way to get more in touch with the physical body and energy.

Look for local meditation classes on the internet or discover them via word-of-mouth. Certain styles of meditation suit different people so you may need to attend different classes to try out different styles. Use your intuition to find the right class.

CHAPTER 12

Opening the Heart

EACH TIME WE HAVE AN awakening experience, we are transformed as if by grace into someone whose heart is more open. Many of our heart-opening moments come about from events in our lives. Things like falling in love, having a baby, losing a loved one, unexpected illness or other highs or lows. All of these events can be triggers for the heart to break open, which helps us get more in touch with our soul.

When we become aware of our soul, we become aware of a number of things.

- That we have been living a life that is not true to our inner self. Sometimes we feel as if we have been in a trance state and suddenly realise there is more to life than we thought.
- Of the oneness of all life and our part in that universal oneness.
- Of a higher power that somehow has an influence on all that is, and we become aware of being part of this higher energy.
- That if we live from soul we can access this higher energy and allow life to flow through us. We may find more direction and become aware of our higher purpose in this life.

All this awareness and awakening happens because our heart is open and our soul takes centre stage in our lives. We don't need to experience tragedy or chaos to open our hearts. We can aim to keep the heart open consciously in a number of ways.

CHOOSING LOVE

One of the best ways to help our hearts remain open is to choose love over fear or hate. When we choose to feel and express love, we open our hearts to the world. Sometimes, choosing love is the hardest path but it will certainly help to bring more light and love into our communities and the world. If we remember to focus on the feeling of love, then we naturally become more heart centred and the energy of love flows through our hearts. It's easy to feel love in some situations but when someone is closed off to us, it becomes harder. This is when it is important to focus on the feeling of love; to really feel it flowing through our heart. Usually, this changes the energy dynamic and the relationship changes and there is increased connection. This energy connection, love, is what binds us together as groups. We all know this feeling of love so we just need to focus on it as much as we can and allow it to flow through us.

AWARENESS OF CLOSING THE HEART

Another way we can live more open-heartedly is to become more aware of when we are closing our hearts. I am aware of this by a heavy feeling in my chest, a feeling of flat energy or a lack of joy in my life. When I forget to be grateful for the abundance in my life or to do more of what lights me up, I start to feel closed off. I may begin to complain or feel flat. As I catch myself in this negative state, I remind myself of all I have and focus on the feeling of love. I begin to open my heart again. I also like to hold the intention to open my heart more often. An intention is an idea that we plan to carry out, and so holding an intention can have great power. When I find myself closing down, I am reminded that what I want is to be more open-hearted. The intention helps me catch myself earlier than I otherwise would and I remember to channel love.

Choosing to live a life full of joy also allows us to open our hearts. Such things as appreciating the beauty around us, listening to music, laughing a lot, being playful, dancing and nourishing our relationships can all bring more joy into our lives. Following our passions and being creative helps us connect with our authentic inner self and this allows us to open our hearts.

When we have been hurt, we are often afraid to be too open-hearted and vulnerable. We don't want to be hurt again. But loving someone or something is the richest part of life. Sure, we will get hurt again because nothing is permanent, and we will lose people we love and pets we love and sometimes things we love. At my lowest points I am always able to remember to open my heart to nature, which helps me get through some very tough times. It's not so strange that the colour of the heart chakra is green so when I'm finding it difficult to open my heart and channel love, I spend more time in nature. This naturally opens my heart and allows me to feel connected again. Even when I'm feeling good, I like to surround myself with plants and their greenness or get out into nature and connect with the earth energies. The sheer beauty of the natural world can open our hearts right up.

In the minimalism chapter, I mentioned letting go of stuff that blocks us, including emotional and mental wounds that block us off from opening the heart fully. When we forgive ourselves for mistakes we have made and let go of blame, we allow our hearts to open more.

When we forgive other people for mistakes they have made, the same thing happens. We are all human and sometimes we do things that hurt other people. Letting go of these hurts can be hard but if we hold onto them, we are blocking our heart energy. Heart wounds can heal if we let go of the blame and look towards love.

GRATITUDE

Being thankful for what we have and practising gratitude are other ways we open our hearts. Sometimes I forget to be grateful for the abundance I have in my life. I may start to worry about money and whether I have enough, and so I close my heart off to receiving. I may start to complain about my work, but I am forgetting to look at what it gives me: the opportunity to make enough money to write and live in a beautiful place and have a lovely house and garden. I am grateful for all those things.

When I make an effort to be grateful for all I have, even things I would rather change, I not only appreciate life more but my energy vibration becomes more positive. As my energy vibration rises, it seems to attract even more positive energy into my life. When I forget to be grateful, I begin to feel more negative and complain more. When I notice I'm moaning about my life, I realise that I have forgotten to practise gratitude for all that I have, which closes my heart.

The energy that flows through our heart flows in as well as out. This energy flow is the critical process in opening our hearts. We open the heart to the energy of the spirit. Spirit exists in everything and it flows as energy through us all. When we open our heart we allow this energy to flow through us.

The heart is the centre. In energetic terms, it is where the soul lives. By living with our hearts open we live a more soulful life and by living a more soulful life we open our hearts. It's a circular rather than a linear process.

LOVE

The process of heart opening is difficult to describe. I have written about ways to help open the heart but it doesn't tell us exactly how to do it. The process is best experienced rather than described.

When we love someone our hearts always crack open, even if it's just a little bit. Heart opening occurs naturally through love. Again, it's a circular process. We love someone, our heart opens a bit; our heart opens a bit, the energy of spirit begins to flow and we feel the love even more. This is the process we are trying to achieve more of the time.

For me, opening the heart is a continual practice. I have to remember to do it. I think some people live with their hearts open all the time and they light up the world with their love and kindness. I have become more used to shielding my heart in order to try and protect myself from hurt, so I have to continually practise heart opening on a conscious level. It's not that I am an unkind person but that much of my kindness is on a thinking level. When I open my heart I become more in touch with my emotions, which seems to me a bit messy sometimes. I am more affected by other people's pain and suffering. I find myself becoming more emotional and crying when I feel other people's hurt.

HEART OPENING AND NEGATIVE ENERGY

For some of us, the world is so full of pain and suffering that we worry we might open our hearts too much and take too much of it in. People who are empathic can be affected by other people's feelings. They often feel drained or depressed due to taking on too much negative energy from other people. I don't think this is because their hearts are too open. I think it is because some empathic people haven't learnt where their boundaries are in energetic terms. The energy overlap between themselves and other people can be too much. This is fine when positive energies are involved, but overlapping our energy field with a very negative person can really affect us. If we are in relationships with negative people, this can be very hard and it often pays to remove ourselves from such relationships. We cannot always fix the relationship or change another person.

In working with people who have negative energy, it is good to keep our heart open but to contract our energetic field to protect ourselves from their negative effects. If we work with people who have had major trauma and are in victim mode where their energy is very negative, we really have to protect ourselves. But this doesn't mean we need to close off our heart. We can keep it open but put up an energetic boundary to keep the negative energies from affecting us so much. Of course if we work with people who have negative energy all the time, we need to use other strategies as well. Some useful strategies include grounding and earthing, meditating and exercise, debriefing and letting go of our emotional reactions. By keeping our hearts open, we can provide positive energy to the relationship, which always has a healing effect.

Opening our hearts is as much about allowing spirit to flow through us as it is about being vulnerable. In many ways, opening our hearts makes us more vulnerable to hurt. This is the human dilemma because on the human level, nothing is permanent and loving will often end in hurt. Yet if we are more aware and conscious, we know that even though nothing is permanent on earth, in the world of spirit love and energy persists.

After my friend Angela died, I could feel her presence around me. I still feel her sometimes and I know her spirit lives on in some dimension. When we feel hurt after someone dies, we need to try to stay open to love despite the loss. We need to live with the pain of loss and know that it is because we are open to love. And we need to work through our emotions until we get to a place where we can open our hearts fully again. This is where we find joy and can live in spirit. This is where our lives are full of magic and wonder.

TOOLS
BOOKS
Resilience from the Heart – Greg Braden. Hay House, 2016. This is about heart-based resilience. It delves into the science behind the heart–brain connection and offers practical strategies to open your heart.

The Heartmath Solution – Doc Childre and Howard Martin. HarperOne, 2011. Provides practical strategies for living from the heart.

THERAPY: BODYWORK, KINESIOLOGY, REIKI
Sometimes we have a really strong blockage in our heart. We may have suffered a great loss or been badly wounded by a relationship break-up. We may be stuck and unable to move forward without help. This is when therapy or bodywork may help release the blockage and allow us to open our hearts more fully again.

Different people respond to different therapy styles. You need to use your intuition as well as your logic to find the style that works best for you. For some people it's talking therapy, for others it's some type of body work therapy and for others, it's energy work such as reiki or kinesiology.

I have a good friend who is a kinesiologist and spiritual healer who can shift blocked energies and bring about amazing healings. She works miracles with her style of therapy and sometimes all it takes is for the client to be willing to undergo a transformation. Being open to change and willing to let blockages be healed helps the process. Finding someone like my friend to help you can be challenging but again, using your intuition and speaking to friends often shows you the path to the right therapist.

TRY THIS

This exercise gets you out of your head and into your heart.

Find a quiet spot and sit or lie comfortably. Take three deep breaths and feel your feet or body connected to the earth. Bring your hands to your heart and shift your focus from your thoughts to your heart space. Feel the energy of your hands pulling your attention to this area. Take a deep breath into your heart space and focus on sending the breath to the heart as you take four more deep breaths.

When you feel more centred in your heart space, bring to your awareness the feeling of love. It may be love for a person or pet. Simply bring this feeling state to the space. Feel the love as you centre your awareness on your heart. You may be aware of your heart beating or the area feeling warm. Stay with the feeling of love and focus it onto the heart space.

Feel your heart space expand and fill with love and light. If you're having trouble feeling love for any reason, try gratitude and focus on that feeling.

As you sit or lie basking in the feeling of love in your heart space, allow the feeling to spread out from the heart and envelop your body, then out beyond your body into your energy field. If you feel like it, send love to whomever you feel may need it at that moment. Feel the expansion of your heart space and its energy.

Then slowly bring your energy back into your field and feel it in your body. Feel your body grounded to the earth and begin to move your fingers and toes. Take three deep breaths as you bring your awareness back to your surroundings. Open your eyes and allow yourself to be present again in a state where your awareness is more in your heart than your head.

This is a great state to be creative in so sometimes, I like to do this exercise before I write. It's especially helpful if I'm stuck or feel blocked. I also like to do it with a clear quartz crystal held over my heart area to amplify the energies and provide healing.

CHAPTER 13

Living in the Present

I LIKE THE IDEA OF living as much as possible in the present moment, but I find it incredibly hard. My mind is so full of thoughts about the past and the future that I often forget that this moment is all that exists right now. When I bring myself into the present moment, I don't have to worry about what is going to happen or what has already happened; I can just be still.

Being present to what is happening right now is a powerful way to get in touch with source energy and our inner selves. We let go of our thoughts about everything and just exist in the spaciousness of the universe. Sounds like it should be easy but it's not. We're so used to believing that our mind, the voice in our head, is who we really are. But we are much deeper and broader than this monologue or dialogue that keeps going around in our minds.

In meditation, we're often able to let go of the thoughts and sink into a deeper experience of reality, but the real trick is to do this in daily life. To make life a spiritual practice we have to continually bring ourselves back to the present moment and let go of our thoughts. When I start complaining or criticising, I realise that I am caught up in my thinking and then I pay attention to this state of mind. When I am worrying endlessly about a problem and then realise that I am stuck in my head again, I try to stop. When my mind is going a million miles an hour or in circles, I can become aware that this is not who I want to be. The critical step is to become aware that I am stuck in my thoughts and no longer present.

The first step in becoming more present is to identify when we are not. Most of us get stuck on this step. We need to pay attention to when we are feeling the discomfort of overthinking or negative thinking and pull ourselves back from it. It is like stepping away from our logical brain for a minute to look at our thoughts as an observer. As we do this, we then have the opportunity to become more present to what is happening.

Becoming Present

Once we have become aware that we are stuck in our thoughts, there are several ways to practise being more present.

First, we deliberately take a step back from our thinking mind and choose to pay attention to the present. We might pay attention to our bodies and the internal sensations, bringing our awareness to any part of our body and paying attention to that part. The mind automatically stops for a while.

A second way is to pay attention to our sense perception; bring our awareness to a tree or the sky and just look without judging or thinking, or pay attention to the sounds that are happening around us.

A third way is to focus on our breathing, the inspiration and expiration, the feeling of the air moving in and out of our lungs.

All these techniques stop the mind from thinking, even if only for a few seconds. They bring us back to the present moment, help us rebalance and let go of mind. It's harder to do this for long periods but it is one of the challenges of transformation – to always be striving to spend more time in the present moment and less time solely in our rational thinking.

The rational thinking mind is mainly where ego resides so when we get stuck in our thinking, we get stuck in ego. When we become more present to life, we begin to live from our inner self and become more whole and more authentic.

Getting stuck in our rational thinking mind is a habit we have all got into. It's a product of the culture we live in, how we have learnt to exist in this culture. We can change but the change is a cultural shift, a paradigm shift. It's shifting from ego-based reality to a reality that is spiritually based.

THE NEW PHYSICS

The spiritual basis is akin to the new physics where everything is connected and is one huge web of energy. When we become present, we tap into this huge web of interconnected energy and so heal our disconnection with source energy and with our inner selves. We become the real person beneath our ego-based exterior and that person/spirit starts to shine through more and more. The more we live in the present and tap into our source the more whole we become. This is what holistic medicine and healing is all about; tapping into our source and staying in touch with that part of us as much as we can, which can bring about healing on all levels.

We can transform our lives when we practise being present.

REALLY PAYING ATTENTION

To be present with other people is to really pay attention to the interaction that is happening in the current moment. Rather than thinking about what has happened in the past or what might happen in the future, we pay attention to the other person right now. Are we listening to what they are saying or are we planning what we will say? Too often, we don't listen to people when we are in conversation. Instead, we are listening to our own thoughts and not connecting with the other person. Listening properly is being present, connecting to the other person and paying attention to what they are saying. Engagement.

Being totally present for another person is very healing. When their story is heard, it somehow resolves and heals things in their mind.

This is part of the healing relationship between a health professional and a patient – if only the health professional can sit still and just be present and listen. Too often the health professional is seeking an answer to some problem that the patient brings, when the real healing often comes when they just listen. The patient feels heard, often for the first time, which can bring about a change in their understanding, which in turn can lead to real healing. I'm not even sure how this works but I've seen it enough times to know it does. You have to let go of the need to find a solution to the other person's problem. You have to trust that they will find their own solution through your being present enough to hear them.

Can this work if we listen to ourselves in the same way? Can we be present for our own self when we have a problem that we are agonising over? Sometimes we can do this through journalling, writing it out, being present to the thoughts and emotions as we write. Not judging ourselves, or the content; just writing it down and paying attention to what comes up.

Of course if we have a tricky problem, then talking to someone who really listens is invaluable, so seeking out people who allow you to be heard is worthwhile. Being with people who are present is healing – if you can find them. But being present to yourself is transformative.

How do we learn to be present?

Or how do we practise it?

PRACTISING BEING PRESENT

Being present in our body is good practice. Paying attention to our breath. Paying attention to our whole body, to where it contacts the earth, to the energy flowing through it, or the energy being blocked. Paying attention to where we are holding tension in our bodies and practising letting that tension go, or letting the emotion go that is holding the tension in. Any form of exercise that brings us back to our body also helps us become present – as long as we are paying attention to our body during the exercise and not just mindlessly exercising.

Some people call it living in the now but we are all living in the now; it's just that our minds aren't always in touch with the now. They're not in the present; they're thinking or worrying about the past or the future. Most of us can't be present all the time. We get some benefit from thinking about the past and the future, reminiscing and dreaming. It is when we worry about the future or agonise over the past that it is not so good. By being more present, we can let go of this mind fullness.

When we find ourselves worrying or thinking negative thoughts, we need to catch ourselves and take our attention from our minds into our bodies, or become more fully aware of the activity that we are undertaking. This is of course the basis of mindfulness – bringing the mind to the task at hand and staying with it. We can practise mindfully washing the dishes or eating dinner or any other activity.

Being present for everyday activities can help with worrying and overthinking, but much of my thinking is more pleasant than paying attention to doing the dishes. Mindfulness can be overrated. I don't think being continually present to every moment is the aim of transformation. I think we're too human and attached to thinking to stop the past and future thinking. I enjoy thinking, analysing, thinking of new ideas or coming to grips with some challenging problem. I don't believe this thinking is what we need to stop. It is when the mind is full of worry, or when we go around in circles and agonise over what we have done or what might happen in some future scenario, that we need to take notice and bring ourselves back to the present moment.

Connect with the present instead of the past or future. Be present to yourself in that sense, when it is needed.

TOOLS
BOOKS
The Power of Now: A Guide to Spiritual Enlightenment – Eckhart Tolle. Hachette Australia, 2011. Eckhart Tolle is the master of being present and this book is a classic. I enjoy his books and also his talks on YouTube or on his website. He is like someone from another planet, or maybe another plane. He makes the practice of being present look easy when it is anything but for most of us.

MINDFULNESS
Most of us have heard about mindfulness practices. They involve bringing your attention to what you are doing or what is happening

in the present moment. They can be used as a form of meditation where you bring your attention to an object or to what your senses are showing you. You might pay attention to what is going on around you with sounds and smells and feelings. You can also use mindfulness by paying attention to an activity like washing the dishes.

I think we can use mindfulness to pay better attention to problem areas of our lives. I am trying to become a mindful consumer by paying attention to my urges to consume and reflect on why I feel a need to buy things that I don't really need. What am I trying to avoid or not feel, how am I caught up in the addiction that is consumerism? When I am mindful about my urges to consume I tend to consume much less.

It is the same with eating. Sometimes I overeat or eat the wrong foods. When I am mindful about eating I pay attention to why I need to eat too much or sugary treats. What need am I trying to fill with food? Am I sad or bored or anxious? I pay attention to how I am feeling and how this is often linked to behaviours I want to stop. When I reach for a glass of wine after a stressful day, I practise mindfulness and begin to look at healthier ways I might de-stress.

Mindfulness is not only about practising being present to the now. It is also about being mindful of our negative behaviours. We pay attention to the patterns and the process. We might not be able to immediately change the behaviours but gradually we notice what we are doing and why. We are paying attention.

CHAPTER 14

Healing

ALL THE TOOLS WE USE in transformation help us to heal on both a physical and a spiritual level. Healing is about becoming whole, which means incorporating all our parts, living a life dictated by heart and soul and spirit. When we are unwell or suffering, this is a sure sign that our soul is trying to get our attention and direct us in a certain way. Instead of looking at illness as a problem, we can look at it as an opportunity to change something about our lives that isn't working for soul and spirit. When we move into alignment with soul and spirit, we can heal many issues. Some health issues are with us for a long time as we learn their lessons. Some health issues we struggle with all our lives. But we can heal ourselves.

It may be that we have to change our lifestyle, or change the way we think, or change the direction of our life. Sometimes we are asked to heal old wounds or confront our shadow. Whatever the health issue is, we are asked to look at the whole self and strip away the ego self to get to our heart and soul self. This inner self can help us heal if we let it.

The inner self will often provide guidance as to how to heal. By following our intuition, we can explore the various ways that soul brings to us. This may be conventional medicine or complementary medicine; it may be exercise or meditation, mindfulness or counselling. It may be quitting a job, doing something we are passionate about, resting more, stepping back from our previous life, ending a relationship or many other actions.

When I had my puff of madness, I tried to work out logically and analyse why it had happened, why I had needed that experience. But I didn't get very far. Two years later, I had another and went through the process again. Both times I became anxious and depressed; a reaction to going crazy I guess. There is such a lack of control when you lose your mind. It's like losing your sense of self and wondering where it has gone. It's as if everything you have built your life on is taken away for a few days. I disappeared and entered another reality. The thinking, logical left side of my brain was disconnected.

I wasn't sure how to avoid another episode. I feared that I would continue to have them and that I had no control over the process. So I had to surrender to my soul's wisdom. It had to have a meaning, if only I could find it. There had to be lessons in the process, if only I could understand them.

For a long time, I couldn't understand why it had happened or what the lesson was. So I took my antipsychotic medication and kept my head down. I continued to write but I knew that I needed to somehow limit myself. I knew I needed to sleep well and not get carried away with ideas too much.

I came to realise that both episodes happened when I was very much in my head; thinking too much about ideas. At the same time, I was filled with fire energy, carried away with ideas that I was passionate about. Both times, I left my body and entered another reality that was to do with my right brain. My upper chakras were whirring with energy but I had forgotten to stay in touch with the earth and my lower chakras and physical body. I floated away from reality.

I've realised quite recently that my lessons are around staying securely connected to the earth energy and not getting completely carried away with ideas. I really need to anchor myself in this physical reality while I explore the other dimensions.

Healing sometimes takes place when we understand intuitively why we have had the illness or disease or symptom. I'm still working out why I needed to go crazy in this lifetime and questioning what it all means. I understand that it helped me see what mental illness is like from the inside, which is very helpful when helping patients. It brought me closer to my family and friends as I had to rely on them for support and ask for help. It led me to look at the needs of my soul in a more complete holistic way. Life, I learnt, wasn't all about passion and light but about dark and connecting to earth energies as well. There are things I saw and felt during the psychotic process that seemed to be messages from another dimension. I remember vividly the otherworldly nature of my experiences. Some of the themes that ran wildly through my brain at the time still resonate in my current life. I have learnt to be a calmer person.

So the healing process for me took many years and involved conventional medicine, taking an antipsychotic, and alternative medicine in exploring the meaning behind my illness and processing that information into different ways of being.

Healing is a natural process; the body is good at it. If we cut ourselves, the skin heals naturally in an amazing way. So too can our other illnesses and diseases heal naturally if we just let our bodies do what they are designed to do. Sometimes we just have to provide a better healing environment by looking after the physical and spiritual dimensions in a more conscious way. To do this, there are a number of steps we can take. I have already written about most of these so the following is a summary.

STEPS TO HEALING

The first step is to take responsibility for our health. This means letting go of the idea that we are victims and looking at the reasons behind our illness, trying to make sense of it and deciding that we can heal ourselves rather than relying upon others to heal us. We can then use our intuition about meaning and management and follow this and the signs towards better health.

The second step is to look after our physical self better, by following a healthy diet and taking herbs or supplements to help us heal. This can be quite a change for some people. There are many healing diets available that the body will welcome. We use our intuition to choose a healthy diet that is right for us, or visit a health professional who can advise on diet and supplements.

The third step is to look after our emotional health by dealing with suppressed or repressed emotional baggage and working on positive emotions. This means letting go of our old stuff and beginning to fill our lives with things that bring us joy and light us up. Letting go of negative emotions can be powerful healing; filling our lives with the positive can be just as therapeutic.

The fourth step is to work on our connections. This includes connections with people, with the earth and nature. Asking for and receiving help can strengthen the bonds we have with family and friends. Being of service to others in some way can help us heal, although many people who are sick have been giving too much of themselves away and need to be more receptive for a while. Connecting with the earth and nature is powerful medicine and should be part of everyone's healing practice.

The fifth step is to take time to work on our purpose and be creative. At the very least, we need to reflect on why we are here and what we can bring to the world. There has to be meaning to our lives and a passion for living. Sometimes we only realise this when we get ill.

All of this leads to the final step, which is to nourish our soul and follow the path of soul. Each of the above steps helps nourish our soul better. We often also need to consciously look at how we have avoided our soul and missed out on the spiritual side of life. Once we pay attention to soul and begin to live from a place that honours soul, then spirit can fill us. This flow of source energy has much healing power.

Look out for my next book, *How to Heal Yourself*, which I aim to publish in 2020 and is a more detailed account of the practical steps people can take to heal themselves.

CHAPTER 15

Tapping into Source Energy

MOST OF WHAT I HAVE written are ways to open our soul and tap into source energy. Tapping into source energy is what inspires us to live our greatest life. It is what brings us into that place of flow where everything seems to be working to our advantage. We feel the energy of source flow through us and out into the world. The energy flows from the earth up through our feet and base chakras. It flows from the sky and heavens down through our crown chakra, and it flows around us. This spirit or source energy is our essence, yet we have forgotten to tap into it.

I feel it flowing strongly when I write, which for me is like channelling wisdom from a place deep inside me that is connected to everything else. This universal wisdom comes from source and spirit but is present in my inner self, my soul, if I can just get into the right space. Tapping into source energy is about getting into the right space.

You can get in the right space in many different ways, and it's important to find your own way. When I write, I pretty easily slip into the space unless I am preoccupied or agonising over something. I find it rewarding to be present, opening myself up to soul and spirit. I don't really know how this happens when I write. Perhaps it is because it's now a habit. I sit at my computer and the words start to flow and I feel in flow. Sometimes it doesn't work quite as well and I might have to leave the writing and do something else. If I do something that connects me to the earth, it usually works well. When I am in flow, I don't think about what I am writing. Rather, I let it flow out of my fingers onto the keyboard. Often, I read back a chapter sometime later and am amazed that I wrote it. It isn't my ego and left brain writing, although they help when I am trying to be more structured and logical.

When I am working at my medical practice, I try to tap into source energy. Sometimes I do but much of the time, I am too stuck in my left brain trying to solve a patient's problem. I strive to be more in touch with source energy at work but old habits die hard so it is a struggle some days. On these days I spend more time centring myself and connecting myself to the earth. When I am in flow, I can connect with the patient on a deep level and seem to know what to say and what questions to ask in order to help them solve their problem.

To centre myself, I focus on my heart and try to open up to my soul. At the same time, I might ground myself by feeling my feet connect to the earth and the earth energy spiral up towards my heart. Sometimes, I use a very earthy crystal like mookaite to ground myself and get myself out of my head and into my body. These strategies help me tap into source energy.

I am very airy usually and too much in my head so the centring and grounding activities bring me back into balance. If you are very earthy, you might need to connect more with the energy of the sky and heaven and open your crown chakra up to source energy. If I do too much of that, I just float away; but someone deeply anchored to the earth might need more connection to the heavens. Very watery or feeling people might need to anchor themselves into their body and ground into the earth. For a fire person who is already channelling energy through their crown chakra, they might need to ground themselves and open their hearts more. It is an individual thing and can change depending upon the situation, but it is good to work out which techniques suit you and help you tap into source energy.

Energy usually flows well when we are doing activities we love, things that light us up and fill us with joy, so it is a good strategy to use to get into flow. We can also tap into source energy by connecting with nature, or by dancing or singing or listening to music or playing a favourite sport. Any creative pursuit will get us in flow. Appreciating beauty and practising gratitude can also get us in flow. We each need to find our own ways to do it best.

Of course, meditation enables us to tap into source energy. We can meditate any way we like as long as it works for us. I use a walking meditation as well as a technique that is specifically for tapping into source energy. This technique only takes about ten minutes each day. It taps into our connection with spirit and opens up our heart and soul. I have included this in the practical Tools section below. If you're not into traditional meditation, this exercise is a good one as a spiritual practice each morning. You may receive intuitive hits when you practise it.

In our three-dimensional way of thinking we often imagine that spirit is something external to us but really, we are part of spirit even though we are currently in human form. Spirit flows through us all the time and the energy waves that make up everything are infused with spirit. We are made up of source energy. I like to think we can open ourselves up to the flow of source energy by tapping into our inner selves. When we are stuck in our heads and egos we are not always open to the flow of energy through us. As we open our hearts and centre ourselves on the inner self/soul, we allow source energy to flow through us. This is when we become more powerfully our true selves. For some people, this may occur most easily when meditating or being in nature, but the real trick in leading a spiritual life is to allow ourselves to be open to this energy flow all the time.

TOOLS
PRACTICE
It's good to practise ways of tapping into source energy every day. Meditation and contemplation are great practices, but the best way I find to tap into source energy is through creativity.

I like to start each day with writing because this is where I can quite easily tap into source energy. While it may take some discipline to get up early and write, it helps me start each day in flow. I begin with something that brings me joy and that channels spirit. What could be better? When I'm able to, I like to spend a greater part of the day writing but even when I am doing my GP work, I still like to start each day in the same way. I let go of my logical thinking and allow myself to be empty. I don't try to think of what to write, it just flows out of me. When I plan, I use my logical brain. When I'm editing my writing, I combine my logic and my intuition. When I write, it comes from some place that isn't logical. It is the same for most creative pursuits; we get out of our left brain and into flow. It's hard to tap into source energy when we are purely in our left brain.

Practise each day tapping into source energy. Meditate. Be creative. Find your joy and passion. As you practise the skill of tapping into source energy in these ways, you will be able to bring it to other parts of your life. You will begin to understand what it feels like to be in flow and to channel spirit, and you can then use it to solve problems and perform miracles.

ENERGY HEALING

Look at the chapter 'Opening the Heart' about energy healing such as reiki and kinesiology for healing blockages, getting your energy flowing better or if you have an illness or disease.

Many energy healers are adept at helping you release trapped emotions, which are effectively blocking the flow of energy in your body. Refer back to the chapter 'Paying Attention to Our Emotions' for help with this.

TRY THIS

Lie on the ground or sit with your feet firmly connected to the earth. This works best outside in nature but can be done inside if you just imagine you are connected to the earth. Close your eyes and take a few deep breaths. Feel your lungs and belly fill with air. Rub your hands together a few times then pull them apart slightly. Feel the energy between your hands for a few moments. Then place your hands on your chest near your heart and feel the energy flow from your hands into your heart. If you are more comfortable, place your hands in your lap.

Next, imagine a stream of light or energy coming from above you, in at the crown chakra, lighting up your head and neck and then moving into the chest. Imagine a similar stream of light or energy coming up through your feet from the earth, rising up the lower chakras to the heart. Imagine both streams of light or energy mixing and moving through you and around you. See yourself surrounded and enveloped by the light as it becomes a sphere around you, streaming through and around you. If you're not great at visualising this as light, you can feel it as energy streaming through your body up from the earth and down from the heavens. As it meets in the heart chakra, it spreads out. As it streams down from above and up from below, it spreads out around you like a sphere of energy. Imagine you are a ball of energy or light connected to the earth, receiving energy or light from above and below. Allow this energy or light to spread out from your heart chakra and imagine the energy connections you have with everyone else. Feel the energy as your heart opens and expands to connect with the people in your inner circle, then the people in your outer circle and beyond.

Sit or lie with this energy moving through you for a few more moments.

Now gradually bring yourself back to your body. Feel your body and its deep connection to the earth. Bring your hands to your lap. Feel the body alive with energy yet deeply connected to the earth. Imagine your energy field contracting back into what is comfortable for you to go on with. Take three deep breaths. Open your eyes and shake out your limbs. Gradually move back into the world.

If you feel spacey or dizzy after this exercise, take some time as you come back into your body to close down the flow of energy a little. Sometimes we are not used to tapping into source energy and the flow is too much, so we need to ground ourselves firmly to the earth and pull the energy into our body, imagining the energy or light slowing and lessening and our aura contracting back into what is comfortable for us. Anchor yourself in your body and ground yourself to the earth.

CONCLUSION

Life is the Spiritual Practice

I LOVE THE CONCEPT THAT life is the spiritual practice. It means I can just live my life without having to spend hours in meditation, prayer or other practices that don't bring me joy. There is no right way to becoming spiritually awake and conscious of our essential nature. The simplest way to do it is to make the whole of life the spiritual practice.

I am committed to transformation and awakening, but it is sometimes hard to let go of my addictive ego thinking and dwell more in spirit. When I write, I find myself being more present and channelling my inner/universal wisdom. But when I go about some of my other activities, I find myself caught up in overthinking. If I am too much in my head, I am not living from my heart and soul.

So for me, the spiritual practice is becoming more aware each time my mind takes over. Not forcing it or fighting it, but simply letting go of my attachment to all those thoughts and surrendering to spirit and the present moment. Surrendering to what is right now.

Right now, I am sitting at a computer typing. It's a beautiful day outside and my mind is telling me I should go outside and enjoy it.

But my inner self is on a roll with the writing so it's the writing that wins.

My writing is a form of channelling universal wisdom. Not for my readers so much as for myself. I learn so much from what I write. It constructs things in a way I can't construct by just using my logical mind. It is more fluid than that. It arises from a place within me that is in touch with universal consciousness and wisdom. Yet my left brain helps in constructing the words and translating the ideas onto paper. I don't know how this process works, and it's beyond my rational control, but it does. I can't always get into flow and write well because sometimes my brain won't give up a train of thought. Or sometimes I get stuck thinking that I don't know what to write. But if I let my thoughts stop and just listen, the words start to come.

I guess this is the way creativity works for most people. The creative process is a part of spiritual practice. It allows the uncensored inner self to shine through. It manifests our authenticity. Our spirit becomes manifest in the works we create and this is part of our divine purpose.

Bringing our authentic self to our creative endeavours is easy in many ways. We get out of our own way to create something wonderful. The rest of our life is just as important, yet in our daily life with friends, family, colleagues and strangers we forget sometimes how to be authentic. We get caught up in the story of our life and the narrative that we construct about who we are. We need to bring our authentic self to the whole of our life.

Who we are is not who we think we are. Those beliefs arise from ego and are another logical construct we build around ourselves. As we become more consciously aware of our real self, we actually need to know less about who we are. The who our ego thinks we are is not the real person, it isn't the essence. It is a belief system we have built up around ourselves over many years.

To deconstruct this belief system and our ego self, we have to turn inwards to our essential nature. We have to let go of the thoughts that control us and allow greater forces to show us how to live. We give up our illusions of control to this greater force. The greater force is not, however, outside of us. It is inside us. It is the essential nature of our very being. We do not need to give up control to a god or deity that is outside of us but rather, to our inner self.

To do this we need to be more in touch with this inner aspect than with our mind and ego. This is the daily practice, the spiritual practice of life. We need to pay attention to when we are not in touch with our inner self. We may be caught up in our minds, removed from being present. We have moved from inner self to mind.

Inner self or soul is really part of the collective consciousness, the timeless part of us all that exists as a drop in the ocean but is also the ocean, not separate from it. It is an illusion that we are all separate. In our human form we seem separate but we are all connected by the energy that is our inner selves. Inner self isn't a physical thing, it is the essence of ourselves that exists outside of time. It isn't a separate thing even though it may appear to be from our human conceptualisation. It is connected to the consciousness of everyone and everything else. It is part of the consciousness of all that is. The parts can't be separate; they are one.

It is hard to explain this in human terms because it isn't logical or rational. But this essential nature is what we are striving to be more conscious of in our lives. We are spiritually awakening by bringing this conscious awareness into our everyday life.

This book is a bit like life. I can't plan it out and then write it, I have to let it unfold as it will. Much of it is not what I expected to write when I started. I keep discovering new things that help me write and experience life in a different way, which is what transformation is all about.

Experiencing life from a different sense of self.

No longer being driven by ego but allowing life to happen as it will.

Surrendering control and being more in the present.

Taking the time to be still in the present moment and not always hurrying on to the next thing.

Living from a different state of consciousness is what it's all about. Yet the old state of consciousness, the ego and the mind, have their grip on us all. It is only with constant practice that we can live from our inner self and soul.

The spiritual practice is about living with a heightened sense of awareness. Being aware of when we are not in alignment with soul and spirit. Being aware of when we fall back into ego habits and step out of flow, and then gently bringing ourselves back to soul centredness and into the flow of spirit.

I realise I am out of flow in various ways that I have described in this book. When I am feeling uncomfortable in body or mind, then soul is asking me to pay attention and probably to change somehow. When life around me seems to be in chaos, it is a sure sign that soul and spirit want me to pay better attention. When I am having trouble with a relationship, the message is always about what I myself might change in the relationship and how I can be more authentic. When I am faced with a crisis, I just need to step back from ego mind and go with the process of allowing my soul to direct me.

Recently, I was stuck in a problem about work and got too stuck in my head when trying to sort out a solution. I had to remind myself to take a step back and try to stop thinking about the outcome so much. I had to remind myself to trust the process and just go with it rather than trying by dint of will and logic to reach a solution.

This situation keeps happening all the time. We get stuck in our heads and ego thinking, especially when we have a problem that brings up our fears and makes us uncomfortable. We forget to trust in spirit and soul and instead return to our old ways of relying upon ego and mind.

This is the spiritual practice: becoming aware of when we let go of our intimate connection to our inner self, to soul and spirit.

I become aware when I realise I am thinking too much about an issue or problem and my brain is hurting. I'm getting better at catching myself early but with this recent problem, it took me a few days to be able to step back and let the process occur naturally rather than trying to control it and plan an outcome. I step back and let spirit guide my actions. I start to pay better attention to the signs and to my intuition. I try to let go of the outcome and just follow the process. As usual, I go back and forth between allowing and trying to control things with my mind. Eventually, the allowing wins and I patiently await the process to occur and an outcome to eventuate; it's just that I don't have control over it.

Some of these lessons of mine are old but I constantly need to remind myself to trust myself, to trust the process of life, to go with the flow and let go of the control over the outcomes. Other people will have different lessons. Mine seem to be about authenticity, trusting life, establishing connections and tapping into my intuition. We are all constantly learning and sometimes relearning how to be more aware and more conscious of our true nature. We tap into this true nature by following the path of soul and stepping into the flow of spirit.

The spiritual practice is this life that we are living.

Simply pay more attention to the whisperings of your soul and you will always find the right path to spirit.

www.ingramcontent.com/pod-product-compliance
Lightning Source LLC
Chambersburg PA
CBHW050435010526
44118CB00013B/1533